The Optimystic's Handbook

THE
OptiMystic's
Handbook

Using Mystical Wisdom
to Discover Hope, Happiness,
and the Wonder of
Spiritual Living

Terry Lynn Taylor &
Mary Beth Crain

HarperSanFrancisco
A Division of HarperCollins*Publishers*

HarperCollins Web Site: http://www.harpercollins.com
HarperCollins®, ♨®, and HarperSanFrancisco™ are trademarks of HarperCollins Publishers Inc.

FIRST EDITION

Library of Congress Cataloging-in-Publication Data
Taylor, Terry Lynn
The optimystic's handbook : using mystical wisdom to discover hope, happiness, and the wonder of spiritual living / Terry Lynn Taylor and Mary Beth Crain. 1st ed.
ISBN 0–06–251465-2 (cloth)
ISBN 0–06–251464-4 (pbk.)
1. Spiritual life. 2. Mysticism. 3. Optimism. I. Crain, Mary Beth. II. Title.
BL624.T4   1997   131–dc21   97-6076

97 98 99 00 01 ❖ RRDH 10 9 8 7 6 5 4 3 2 1

This book is dedicated to the memory of Mary Beth's beloved husband, Adam Shields, who died during the writing of it. Adam's quiet courage in the face of terminal illness was the ultimate lesson in optimysticism. His irrepressible sense of humor and gratefulness for life often reminded us that an optimystic approach to living is entirely possible and appropriate, even in the midst of deepest pain and sorrow. Through his death, both of us gained a renewed appreciation for life and the mystical resilience of the human spirit.

Contents

Acknowledgments

The authors would like to thank a number of people at Harper San Francisco who made *The Optimystic's Handbook* possible: Tom Grady, for his optimystic vision in buying it; their editor, Lisa Bach, and her assistant, Laura Harger, for their optimystic trust that the manuscript, though late, was really going to be finished and would really be as good as we'd promised; our copyeditor, Priscilla Stuckey, for her excellent suggestions and optimystic feel for the manuscript; and our production editor, Mimi Kusch, for her optimystic enjoyment of the project. We would also like to thank our agent, Loretta Barrett, for her much-appreciated editorial input and her optimystic support of our ideas and our gifts; her assistant, Karen Gerbach-Stoopak, for her heroic work in the line of duty; "Wildman" Ray Hart for getting us an emergency copy of *Desiderata* off his bathroom wall; Terry's significant other, Joe Kelly Jackson, for his love, support, sense of humor, and appreciation of the optimystic significance of just being here; the staff of Starbuck's in Ventura, California, for providing a great space for writing and creating; and all of Mary Beth's friends and family who helped her through her husband's illness and death while cheering her on to finish this book and prove the optimystic truth that sorrow is often the first step toward wisdom, and death, oddly enough, can be the first step toward life.

The Optimystic's Handbook

O
I

What Is Optimysticism?

Optimysticism is the choice we make not only to experience the best of this world but also to see beyond this world, into eternity, and in so doing to live the mystery to the fullest here on earth.

Chances are quite good that if you are reading this, you are a human being living on planet Earth. Chances are also quite good that some days you've wondered if you even belong on Earth. With all its misery, uncertainty, and seemingly unbridled chaos, this obstreperous child of the vast cosmos can't be all there is for us. Can it?

But the very fact that you have picked up this book indicates that hope is an essential part of your outlook. You know that life can be tough, but you also know that it can be glorious. And you are a risk taker at heart, for somehow you just wouldn't trade the fascinating unpredictability of this existence for the platitudes of a zombie life. You know that your humanness is a gift; you probably have had moments of ecstasy in which you were suddenly immersed in the love of creation, feeling a soul-stirring part of something far greater than yourself. You may also have had psychic flashes or experienced inexplicable synchronistic miracles that have beckoned you into another dimension, past logic, into heart, soul, inner knowing.

Congratulations. You have chosen not to sleepwalk through life. You are awake—and yearning to be truly alive. You know that there is far more to life than just the physical dimension; you know that there is a higher purpose that, when you discover and heed it, will lead you past where you thought your limits were into a realm of passionate commitment to all that is and all that is yet to be.

Yet perhaps, at the same time, a fear has held you back—the fear of accepting all that this life has to offer, not just physically but spiritually. If so, you have plenty of company. We are all creatures of paradox, dependent upon the physical plane for our survival, yet yearning for the metaphysical tools to become truly *alive* on this Earth. We are torn between wanting security and wanting to break free, between deadening ourselves to the pain of life and opening ourselves up to the experience of living, between racing to protect our future and standing still to enjoy the moment, between *surviving* and *thriving*.

But how do we get there from here? How do we find what we are seeking? And what do we do with it once we have found it?

What we are looking for is optimysticism. What we can do with it once we have found it is to live—more fully, more honestly, more hopefully than we perhaps ever dreamed was possible.

The Brave New World of Optimysticism

Optimysticism is the choice we make not only to experience the best of this world but also to see beyond this world, into eternity, and in so doing to live the mystery to the fullest here on Earth.

The word *optimysticism* obviously has many fascinating possibilities. If we break the term down, we find that the root, *opt*, comes from the Latin *optare*, "to choose." *Opt* is also the root of *optic*, "to see," and *optimum*, "the best"; this is the definition of *optimism*, seeing the best of something. *Mysticism* comes from the Greek *mystikos*, or "mystery"; the earliest definition of a mystic was one who was initiated into the "mysteries," a realm of secret, holy knowing that revealed a world beyond that which is accessible to the five ordinary senses alone. As F. C. Happold remarks in his book *Mysticism: A Study and an Anthology*, mysticism can be thought of as "a break through the world of time and history into one of eternity and timelessness." The word *mystery,* in turn, derives from the Greek verb *muo,* which means to "shut the senses," to close the lips or eyes. Thus, *muteness* would come from *muo,* and silence would be its companion. But we are not speaking here of the isolation and rigorous asceticism of the vow of silence to which certain monks and ascetics bind themselves. Rather, the silence of the optimystic is the silence of wonder, as we pause to listen to the world's heartbeat and the call of our own soul.

But perhaps the key word here is *choice.* We all have the choice, here and now, to become optimystics. We can all "opt" for a new way of seeing that involves a type of expanded vision almost miraculous in its depth and scope. This vision entails all the dimensions of the term *vision,* which can mean sight itself, both outer and inner, or a dream of a goal to reach and a higher purpose to fulfill, or the perception of otherworldly phenomena and spiritual experience. If the optimist sees with two eyes, the optimystic sees with three—the two "outer" eyes and the inner or "third" eye, the center of our spiritual awakening, the true visionary apparatus. Thus, optimystic vision is a seeing of limitless dimensions. Through *The Optimystic's Handbook* you will learn how to see the world, yourself, and your problems and potential with new eyes, as you begin to experience for yourself the delightful truth that *in the realm of the mysteries, all things are possible.*

Above all, optimysticism is a new way of answering the six basic yearnings we all share as human beings:

1. *Joy.* We were born with the capacity for total joy. Unhappiness and fear are learned responses; joy is spontaneous and unconditioned.

2. *Vitality.* We want to feel energy and power coursing through our veins, stimulating our senses, filling us with curiosity, wonder, and, above all, a passion for living.

3. *Meaning.* We want meaning and purpose in our lives. We don't want to feel that we were created by accident, that we don't matter, that what we do has no effect on the world. We want to feel important and vital; we want a purpose to give us direction and fulfillment.

4. *Peace.* We want, as much as possible, to be free of pain and worry.

5. *Love.* We want to love and be loved.

6. *A spiritual foundation.* We want to have a relationship with the universe that extends beyond ourselves into a unity with all things, giving us a sense of transcendence that helps us to brave tragedy and suffering and discover an internal, eternal core of stability and peace.

Now the optimist says: My life is joyous and vital. It has meaning and purpose. I prefer to create rather than to worry, to look for joy rather than to wallow in pain. I find love wherever I choose to look for it.

But the optimystic says: My life is joyous and vital *because it is an integral part of something far greater than myself.* I find joy and meaning in my life through union with the Thing That Is Greater Than Myself. I extend beyond this body, beyond this time frame, into eternity. I do not worry, for I know that I am greater than this physical self and that therefore this physical self has no real power over me. I experience the love of God that is in everything and therefore in me; knowing that I am so loved, I can love others in the same way, without fear. Thus, if the optimist has the best of this world, the optimystic has the best of both worlds—spiritual and material, physical and metaphysical, the here and the hereafter.

Think about it for a moment. Do you have all the ingredients for satisfaction—joy, vitality, meaning, peace, love, and a strong spiritual foundation—in your life? If so, congratulations. If not, what do you suppose are the reasons happiness or love or serenity or excitement or a strong sense of aliveness have eluded you? Where are the holes in your life, the places waiting to be filled?

As the Amish quilters will make sure that each quilt contains a mismatched patch, which not only reminds them of their own imperfections but becomes, they believe, the space through which the spirit enters the creation, so the optimystic regards the holes in life in terms not of emptiness but of potential. That which is missing affords us the opportunity for fulfillment, urging us to reconnect to our deepest source, the realm of imagination, intuition, and spirit, for guidance and insight. The optimystic is always attuned to the right-brain forces behind the left-brain throne, the higher reaches of consciousness that are the source of our true power not simply as human beings but as everlasting souls.

This, then, is a book about learning to welcome the emptiness so that we can make room for the spirit. Optimystics are not afraid of space or silence, for they know that these are often direct avenues to the mysteries. In *The Optimystic's Handbook,* you will learn how to work with space and silence in order to reach new levels of awareness and inner power, and you will learn how to turn the negative energy of frustration and unhappiness into the positive energy of passion and aliveness. For, ultimately, optimysticism is a process of *attunement* to messages from the soul that help us open to the powerful forces of renewal and transformation that are always available to us. Optimystics *respond* to life. They do not try to control it so much as listen to it. As such, optimysticism is a process as well as an attitude, a constantly growing, constantly changing *experience of life.*

Debunking Myths About Optimism and Mysticism

The average person regards both optimism and mysticism with suspicion, as diversions from reality. Many people view optimism as an unrealistic, candy-coated approach to life and mysticism as an esoteric exercise in renunciation of the material world meant for only the odd, chosen few. But nothing could be further from the truth. Both optimism and mysticism are not only realistic approaches to life, they are quite possibly the only practical attitudes to take in a world over which we have no control, a world that can turn on us at any moment and send us spinning into the far reaches of desolation, a world in which suffering, injustice, and downright unfairness are seemingly the rule, not the exception.

This is why pessimism so often has been confused with realism, optimism with denial, and mysticism with escape. How can one be an optimist in a world in which innocent children are abused and murdered every day? How can one be a mystic in a world that God must have deserted long ago? It is the pessimist who is the realist, who sees the thorns where the optimist sees only the rose, and the mystic, according to this view, sees nothing at all, being so absorbed in an inner reality that transcends the physical world.

But to equate pessimism with realism is "optimythicism." In *reality,* the optimist sees both the rose and the thorns but chooses to concentrate on the rose. The mystic sees the beauty and divine creative genius in both the rose and the thorns. It is the poor pessimist who sees only the thorns and who subsequently runs from life in an effort to avoid them at all costs.

There is nothing unrealistic or illusory about either optimism or mysticism. In fact, both equip the human being with the power to live more fully, more completely, more in the now. In many studies done by psychologists at Harvard University and the University of Michigan on optimistic versus pessimistic personalities, it has been discovered, again and again, that optimists tend to approach life actively—that is, in a positive, goal-oriented manner—while pessimists tend to remain more passive, victim identified, and therefore ultimately are less prone to achievement.

Similarly, the true mystic does not reject life but rather celebrates every aspect of its being. Mysticism is not something above and beyond ordinary human experience; the true mystic is not a strange being having one foot in heaven and the other on a banana peel. No; the true mystic *sees the extraordinary in the ordinary and appreciates the miraculous in all things great and small.* The spirit of mysticism is the spirit of celebration. It rejoices in the mystery of creation and in the union of the soul not only with God but also with all living things. Because mysticism is a quest for union with God, it automatically implies a hopeful view of our spiritual quest on—and beyond—the Earth.

Becoming Optimystic in Today's World

A lot of people today are suffering from PMS—Pre-Millennial Syndrome. As they approach the doorstep of the twenty-first century, they are beset with apocalyptic apprehension. Nostradamus, the Hopis, the Mayans, and many other ancient sources, they say, predicted cataclysmic upheaval by the year 2000. Such predictions have caused many of us to question the very notion of a future for ourselves, our children, the entire human race. After all, with genocide, child abuse, domestic violence, and everyday wanton drive-by killings being just a few of the nightly news topics, our current world often seems to be unable to answer our most basic human needs for comfort, safety, and hope.

But we must be aware of the fact that things really are no worse now than they always have been. A hundred years ago, for instance, women in many American cities were just as afraid as they are today to venture out onto the street because rape was so common. Children were abused openly or, incredible as it may seem, were forced to work sixteen-hour days at the age of three. People were defenseless against illnesses and epidemics that limited the average lifespan to around thirty-seven years. And as for the romantic image of the secure two-parent family of the past, well, perhaps divorce was far less common because people didn't live long enough to get fed up with each other! In other words, romanticizing the past is a genuine waste of time. The best we can do with history is to learn from it, not revere it. The only difference between then and now is that with the help of technology we are far more aware of the misery going on in the rest of the world, and we are better able to self-destruct more quickly and efficiently than we were a century or even a half-century ago.

Many of us today are asking, How can anyone possibly be an optimist—let alone an optimystic—in the face of the atrocities and terrors before which we stand helpless and overwhelmed? But this is exactly the world in which optimysticism works best. Why?

Because when we become optimystics, we acquire the survival tool of *compassionate detachment.* We may see with open eyes, we may do what we can to help the situation, but we do not become overwhelmed by circumstances. As optimystics, we see from above, not from below. With our expanded optimystic vision, we grasp the larger picture and thus are better able to put things in their proper perspective. At the same time, we are never so far removed from reality as to be cold, uncaring, and aloof from another's pain. Instead, as optimystics we offer a presence that can lift the spirits and change the perspective of others. We do not have to *do* so much as *be,* radiating a peaceful awareness that can alter the vibrations of the universe and turn others toward the light—their own light.

In fact, optimysticism just may be our only antidote to the current state of the world because it *redefines the nature of our experience.* It does not deny reality; it simply chooses to see the beauty of a larger destiny and to help others rise to the level of that beauty. The optimystic knows that the search for beauty is the most noble of all causes. As radical theologian Matthew Fox asserts, mysticism is rooted in "our capacity for enjoyment—our search for the beautiful and its search for us." The optimist expects the best possible outcome; the optimystic has already experienced it, by the very nature of his or her relationship to divine love.

Above all, optimystics do not buy into statistics. The media continually bombards us with negative information and predictions. But we tend to forget that the images and statistics being fed to us are incredibly selective. They are only part of the picture, the results of choices in reporting motivated by the intention to frighten and shock rather than educate and inspire. When we find ourselves succumbing to the fear that such dismal scenarios engender, we can make the choice to remember two things: (a) the statistics are only one aspect of reality; and (b) we have the power at all times to create our own reality. Statistics are always being proved wrong; impossible dreams have the curious habit of coming true. We hear and read about uplifting reports too, but they are not emphasized in our society to nearly the same degree of intensity. So we simply have to emphasize them ourselves.

The Light of the World

I never knew the sun to be knocked down and rolled through a mud puddle; he comes out honor bright from behind every storm.

Henry David Thoreau

People often view mysticism as retreat—into the ineffable silence where the soul speaks most clearly, into the dark night of the soul where one wrestles with the silence that sometimes becomes a terrifying emptiness. But mysticism also has its daylight side. It is significant that the Christ spirit is referred to in the New Testament not as "the dark night of the soul" but as "the light of the world." The true mystic—one who is one with God—is a being and a messenger of light and lightness, in both heart and spirit. The optimystic is a firm believer in the sunlight, knowing that it is always there even when obscured by the clouds and that its rising is a given even when it is overtaken by night.

This is more than simplistic positive thinking, although positive thinking is an essential ingredient of optimysticism. The optimystic observes, clearly and faithfully, the dovetailing of the human and natural life cycles. Natural laws, which support us when we live in harmony with them, apply also to human nature. For instance, our moods do not define us but are passing, like clouds; our spirit, like the sun, can never be knocked down and rolled through a mud puddle but is, instead, always there, illuminating our path; no matter how dark the way may seem at one moment, daylight not only can but will break upon it the next. When we realize this, we move upward, beyond the confines and limitations of our day-to-day lives, toward the sunlight of the immortal, ever-resurrecting soul that is our true self.

Starting Out on the Optimystic Path

Becoming an optimystic is as complicated or uncomplicated as you choose to make it. Choice derives from *opt,* remember? You can decide that you have "all this work to do," spiritual and otherwise, before you are pure and holy enough to embark upon the optimystic path. You can decide that you have to face your demons first, that you have to do miles of digging into the center of your psyche in order to unearth all the unconscious debris clogging up your conscious life before you can be truly happy enough to accept optimysticism as a way of life. You can wrestle until doomsday (and you will, take our word for it) over sticky moral or theological issues like the nature of evil and the inevitability of pain and why nobody really deserves to be totally happy and at peace in a world brimming over with every conceivable kind of suffering. Or you can simply decide, right here and now, to throw intellectual caution to the winds and just go for it, optimystically speaking.

Should you select the last *opt*ion, we suggest that you take as little with you as possible. In other words, leave your preconceptions and former belief systems behind; they'll only add a lot of extra weight to your psychic backpack. Remember, the song of the open road begins with an open mind. Make the choice here and now to see things with the eyes of a child, to let the mystery unfold, to let yourself experience wonder, to live each day not as if it were your last, but as if it were your first. This is the first step in becoming an optimystic.

Besides an open mind, some of the other things you'll need to take with you are:

1. Hope

2. Humor

3. Dreams

4. An appreciation of mystery

5. Occasional quiet time and space

6. Gratitude

7. Adaptability

8. Expectation

9. A light heart

10. Trust

These items are the ten basic keys to happiness, for each one of them opens a door to higher consciousness that may have been closed until now. But don't expect to have these keys on hand immediately. *The Optimystic's Handbook* is a guide to incorporating these vital qualities in your life. As you read it, we hope you will become more and more of an optimystic, until one day you reach into the pocket of your consciousness to find all ten of them on your key chain. And at that glorious moment you'll know that you can never be locked out of life again.

Discovering Your Optimystic Quotient

Most of us go through life on automatic pilot, taking certain beliefs and reactions so much for granted that we may be oblivious not only to *why* we are behaving or feeling a certain way, but also to the fact *that* we are subscribing to certain ways of experiencing the world.

In breakthrough studies on optimistic versus pessimistic personalities conducted by renowned psychologists Martin Seligman, Lyn Abramson, and John Teasdale at the University of Pennsylvania in 1978, the term *explanatory style* was used to describe how we tend to explain things that happen to us. For instance, if a pessimist doesn't get the job he has interviewed for, he will tend to interpret the event as follows: "That interviewer hated me as soon as I walked in the door. That always happens. I never make a good impression. I'm always goofing up at interviews. This was the job I'd been waiting for, and I blew it. I'll never get the job I want." This is known as a "personal, pervasive, and permanent" explanatory style. The pessimist takes personal responsibility for all the failures, real and imagined, in his life. He will see one failure as representative of his entire life, and he will regard failure as a permanent condition that he is powerless to change.

But if an optimist doesn't get the job, by contrast, she might reason, "I didn't respond well to certain questions at the interview. I usually do really well at interviews; this just wasn't my day. But there are plenty of other jobs out there; it's just a matter of connecting with the right one." This is known as an "impersonal, impermanent, and specific" explanatory style. With this attitude, the optimist doesn't take the rejection personally, she sees the setback as temporary, and she is able to regard this particular failure as an isolated incident, not as a measure of her entire life.

But what about the optimystic explanatory style? If the optimist takes an impermanent view of setback and a pessimist takes a permanent one, the optimystic's explanatory style is *transcendent*. If an optimystic applies for a job and doesn't get it, he or she might say, "Okay. This job wasn't meant to be. I surrender to the bigger picture, to a higher power, to the unseen forces that are guiding me and shaping my destiny. I trust that I took advantage of this opportunity for a reason that will be revealed to me in its own time." As such, the optimystic really prefers not to have any explanatory style at all, for explanations can be both unnecessary and limiting. If, as psychomythologist Sam Keen observes, *to explain* means "to lay out flat," getting rid of the mountains and valleys, the optimystic seeks to go beyond explanations, to follow the lead of the mystery. The optimystic is the true explorer of life, climbing to the top of the mountains of visionary awareness and exploring the very bottom of the valleys of the unconscious without trepidation.

An integral part of the optimystic approach to life is the ability to notice beauty and meaning around us while at the same time being able to laugh at ourselves and at the comedy of errors that is sometimes referred to as life. The laughter comes when we are willing to let go of the crippling seriousness of self-judgment and let our optimystic nature take the stage.

How much of a natural optimystic are you? What is your current attitude toward life, yourself, and God? What is your explanatory style—your pattern of viewing setbacks and successes, losses and gains in your life? How simple have you made your life? How do you respond to sunsets, children, and animals? How much of a place in your life have you made for silence and reflection? For pleasure? For laughter? Are you in the habit of spiritual self-renewal, or are you due for a spiritual tune-up?

All of us are optimystics to some degree. The inner review that follows is designed to help you rate your personal outlook on life and to see where you are on the optimystic scale. It is not a test; there are, of course, no right or wrong answers, so cheating can't get you a better grade. Just answer honestly, and enjoy the process of self-discovery! When you are ready to begin, relax, breathe deeply, center yourself, and take the review in an atmosphere of peace, quiet, and gentleness. We also suggest that you do this review again when you have finished reading *The Optimystic's Handbook* and that you return to it periodically, perhaps every few months, as an exercise in awareness and an affirmation of how you are continually changing and growing.

The Inner Review

Answer the following questions with a number from 1 to 5 that best describes you.

> 1 = Never
>
> 2 = Rarely
>
> 3 = Sometimes
>
> 4 = Often
>
> 5 = Always

1. Do you welcome change and feel comfortable with it?

2. Do you spend time in prayer and/or meditation?

3. Do you stop to admire flowers?

4. How often do you stop to have a conversation with a child?

5. Do you try to communicate with animals?

6. How often do you stop to wonder at the sky?

7. Do you adopt the philosophy of taking things lightly?

8. Do you feel grateful for life?

9. Do you ever have peak experiences of ecstasy?

10. How often do you find the humor in situations?

11. When you feel confused or worried about something, are you able to trust in a higher power to help you through your difficulty?

12. When reading a mystery, does your enjoyment come from the mystery itself?

13. How often do you feel passionate about something?

14. How often are you able to keep your center when things around you seem to be falling apart?

15. Do you find more virtue in happiness than suffering?

16. How often do you wish on a star, a moonbeam, or a rainbow?

17. How often do you see beyond popular explanations held by your social group?

18. How often do you call in sick to work just because you need a day of fun?

19. Do you find enjoyment in little things?

20. Do you respect your intuition?

21. How often are you willing to accept pain in your life as a teacher rather than a tormentor?

22. Do you keep an open mind, even when you don't understand something?

23. Do you take the time to remember others in little ways?

24. How often do you ask for—and expect—a miracle?

25. How often do you believe that you have the right to live a peaceful and happy life, even in the midst of disaster and sorrow?

26. How often do you believe that you have the power and the responsibility to bring joy and meaning to the lives of others?

27. Are you aware of and attuned to the cycles of nature?

28. When it's gray and gloomy out, do you still take time to appreciate the more subtle beauty of the sky, the moods of the clouds, the coolness of the air?

29. Do you put a high premium on pleasure?

30. How often do you experience good old-fashioned synchronicity?

31. Do you leave perfectionism to God?

32. Regardless of your age, do you feel young?

33. Do you ever think about the reason that you are here?

For the following questions, choose the answer that is most appropriate.

34. When you watch the latest disasters on the six o'clock news, are you prompted to:

    A. Build a coffin and climb in?

    B. Accept the fact that suffering is our lot on Earth?

    C. Pray to God for things to get better?

    D. Turn immediately to the cartoons?

    E. Continue to live your own life as meaningfully as possible?

35. If your neighbor came by and told you he'd just built a spaceship and was going to the moon tomorrow and would you like to come along, would you:

    A. Ask him if he'd put a little too much LSD in his morning coffee?

    B. Worry about whether there'll be a place on the moon to buy toothpaste?

    C. Run right out to go shopping for the latest in moon fashions?

    D. Say, "Sure!"?

    E. Say, "Sure, but we don't need a spaceship!"?

36. When your soul tries to speak to you, do you:

    A. Turn on your Walkman extra loud?

    B. Tell yourself that you're just imagining things?

    C. Ask if it can call back later?

    D. Stop to listen?

    E. Invite it in for coffee?

Your Personal Evaluation

Count up your points, giving yourself one point for all the A answers on the last three questions, two points for Bs, three points for Cs, four points for Ds, and five points for Es.

If your numbers tallied:

185–160: Congratulations. Your Optimystic Quotient is exceedingly high. You have a healthy degree of enjoyment and appreciation for life; you feel connected to God, nature, and your soul; you are compassionate and passionate; you take responsibility for your higher purpose on earth; and you know how to have fun.

159–130: Very good. You are well along on your optimystic journey. At times you may feel more doubtful than trusting in the power of divine love and in your own spiritual resources, but you are ultimately saved by your open mind.

129–90: Oh-oh. Are you a mystic fence sitter? It seems as though you're having a little trouble deciding if life is infinitely beautiful or just a place to hang out. You've got what it takes, but you need a good dose of trust and faith.

89–60: Is it possible that you've been denying your mystic self? If so, let this be your encouragement to start looking for and believing in the possibility of ecstasy.

59–37: Danger! Diminishing optimystic pulse! Call in the life-support systems! But remember, it's never too late to let passion, enthusiasm, love, generosity, humor, trust, peace, and joy into your life.

2

Awakening to Your Mystic Self

For now is the hour when we are in danger of forgetting for what purpose we are on earth.

HERBERT WEINER, *9 1/2 MYSTICS: THE KABBALA TODAY*

Awakening to our mystic self means awakening to the reason that we were brought to Earth, remembering why we are here. For our soul knows the reason and has always known it, but our ego has been asleep. Even though we think we have been awake, knowing the difference between waking and sleeping, in truth we are all sleepwalkers on the Earth until we have awakened to our inner life. The words of the Persian poet and mystic, Kabir, ring like the first church bells of the morning, rousing our souls from the slumber of life:

> Friend, wake up! Why do you go on sleeping?
> The night is over—do you want to lose the day
> the same way?
> Others who have managed to get up early have
> already found an elephant or a jewel . . .
> So much was lost already while you slept . . .
> And that was so unnecessary!

Your mystic self remembers why you are here. It is no accident that you were born. Awakening to your mystic self will awaken you to your purpose, your potential, your power as a single human being to shape your destiny and affect the lives of others. You are not inconsequential; on the contrary, every attitude you adopt, every action you take, matters. The mystic in you knows that everything you do, say, or think has consequences.

The knowledge that everything matters has been known to lead to a burdensome sense of responsibility laced with guilt. The concept of sin is well known in Catholicism, which urges its followers to confess not only things considered to be sinful actions and thoughts, but also things one should have done but didn't. Certain Buddhist teachings warn that you can spend hundreds of thousands of years in umpteen levels of hell for your negative thoughts and actions and your wasted years of spiritual negligence. Optimysticism, however, takes a happier view of the situation. The optimystic doesn't live in fear of what he or she should have done but didn't or in fear of what eternity holds if we don't clean up our act now. The optimystic is ecstatic at the thought that he or she has been given this marvelous power of consequence, that as mere individual human beings, no more than flickers on the cosmic screen, we actually have the ability to transform the world, inside and out.

Transformation begins with the self. And the first step in transformation is waking up. But what does being awake really mean? The origin of the word *awake* is the old English *wacan*, which referred to a watch or vigil. In Buddhism, being awake means being free of *samsara*, life's illusions that parade as reality. *Samsara* is the great deceiver; when we are in its grasp, we believe in the permanence of the physical body, we become prisoners of the chains of desire that bind us to the material world, and we are drawn into the great web of suffering that inevitably results when we are attached to outcomes over which we really have no control. When we are awake, however, we understand that the physical world is not the be-all and end-all of existence; we know that our true self, our "nature mind" is immortal and eternal, that we are part of everything and that everything is part of us, that there is no separation between us and God, and so there is absolutely no reason for us not to be filled with joy.

The Mystery Is the Magic

We often hear people talk of "transcendent experience." But what exactly is a transcendent experience? In most religions and cultures, the mystic is revered as one who has been initiated into the mysteries. The mysteries—which remain just that to the average person—involve a transcendence of the physical plane that leads to direct union with something called God. This transcendent experience invariably produces a state of joy and ecstasy, as the experiencer soars beyond the ego and past the physical boundaries by which human beings so doggedly persist in defining the self. A transcendent experience involves a consciousness not only of something far greater than the self, but also of the marvelous fact that we are actually part of that greater something, that we exist above and beyond our fragile temporal body. Mystics of every religion— Hindu, Sufi, Jewish, Christian, Buddhist, Muslim, whatever— speak of the profound bliss that comes with truly awakening to our larger nature, our infinite self, the oneness of everything. No longer are we imprisoned in a finite identity. No longer are we alone, separate from our fellows and our maker. We *are* our fellows; we *are* our maker. We are all, and we are endless. What a magical, liberating realization!

This awakening can come through practiced meditation, or it may take the form of a sudden, completely unexpected flash of insight that hits in the midst of the most mundane activity. Psychologist William James had a mystical experience as a Cambridge undergrad. While he was sitting in his dorm room on a perfectly ordinary evening, he suddenly felt a mysterious presence that took him out of himself and into a state of "unbearable joy," followed by a "deep sense of peace, security, and certainty." Others have had mystical experiences during walks or while playing sports.

You yourself may have had a transcendent awakening when you least expected it. And why not? Your mystic self thrives on the elements of surprise and mystery.

When we think of a mystery, we think of something unknown that needs to be solved. But our mystic self is far more at home with the mystery itself. The famous fourteenth-century anonymous treatise on mysticism, *The Cloud of Unknowing,* is a celebration not of the known but of the unknown on the mystic path, for the unknown is the place where, free of preconceptions, we can be open to true discovery and true magic. Your mystic self does not try to control events but instead allows life to unfold. It reveres the inexplicable, for it is most often through what cannot be explained that we finally meet God, in a state not of knowing it all but of surrendered trust. There is nothing more magical than this, the merging of human and divine, the finding of the true self in the supreme act of letting go of the false one.

Who, or what, is this mystic self? What are some of its characteristics?

Your mystic self:

1. *Feels at one with the universal life force.* It does not feel separate from others or from anything, especially God.

2. *Knows that it is timeless.* Death has no meaning to your mystic self, except as departure from the physical house. Your mystic self knows it cannot die.

3. *Rejoices in the beauty and perfection of the universe, even in the midst of suffering.* Your mystic self is able to move naturally in the realm of compassion without becoming weighted down by sadness, because it knows that suffering is a gift that can open us to the freedom of the higher realms. Through suffering we are forced to ask questions we might have otherwise avoided, such as "What's the meaning of life?" and "Why is this pain necessary?" These questions can help us open up to our mystic—our endless—self and thus move us beyond suffering into the real experience of living.

4. *Expands with life instead of contracting with fear.* Your mystic self is huge; the more life it feels, the larger it becomes. Your mystic self is

passionate and creative, fully involved in exploring, interacting with, and celebrating life.

5. *Is physically based and metaphysically directed.* Being mystically awake does not mean we have to go into an altered state. On the contrary, the real mystic should ideally be more grounded, more in tune with the Earth, because mysticism is really the most alive approach to life that we can take. True mysticism incorporates the whole (holy) person— body, mind, spirit, soul—into the challenge of living. Everyone is a mystic. Why? Because mysticism is nothing less than experience—the experience of life. Not past life or the afterlife, but the present life, the one we received from God for some particular but unarguable reason at this moment in time.

6. *Loves a good mystery.* Your mystic self knows that trying to explain, predict, and control life is futile. It doesn't mind in the least being surprised by life; in fact, it regards education as the learning that takes place through spontaneous encounters with the unexpected. Your mystic self takes the road less traveled—the road that leads directly into the unknown and into the soul's awakening and fulfillment.

7. *Is always in love.* Your mystic self radiates love and, like a magnet, draws love back to itself. Your mystic self is healthy; studies have proven the positive effect being in love has on illness. People are often healed, physically and emotionally, through love.

8. *Knows how to want what it has.* Your mystic self appreciates everything it has been given, good and bad, for in reality it does not perceive anything as either good or bad but simply part of the divinely planned process.

9. *Sees God as its playmate.* Your mystic self is not afraid of, intimidated by, or disbelieving of God. Instead, it and God are best friends, for it knows that they are part of each other.

10. *Knows how to trust.* Your mystic self understands that often things happen for reasons that are not immediately apparent and that the best way to approach the uncertainties of life is to welcome them. It knows that God is always present, even when fear puts up a roadblock, and it knows also that when the heart is full of expectation, prayers will always be answered *on the deepest level of need.* The thing we initially ask for may not be granted, but our mystic self knows that we are always given what we need, in ways we might not have imagined.

In case you haven't already realized it, *you are your mystic self.* As the Buddhists say, we are all the Buddha, for the Buddha is nothing more than the realization of the universal nature mind of which we are all a part. If you feel separate from your mystic self, it is only because you have not allowed yourself to open to what is already there. So take a moment now to review the ten basic qualities of your mystic self. Which ones do you automatically connect with? Which ones do you feel alienated from? Make a list of each, and reflect upon why some of these aspects of your mystic self—your own self—might be more of a reality to you than others.

If we go back to the origin of *awake* in *wacan,* or keeping vigil, awakening to our mystic self involves being alert for signs of it, keeping a vigil over it until it emerges from the fog of our illusions of ego and separateness. We see, with a welling up of gratefulness in our hearts, that our mystic self was really there all along, patiently waiting for us to stumble upon it.

And stumble we do. The Indian sage Meher Baba maintained,

> Man does not usually turn to a real search for God as a matter of voluntary and joyous enterprise. He has to be driven to this search by disillusionment with those worldly things which allure him. . . . In the moment of such divine desperateness a man makes the important decision to discover and realize the aim of life.

Perhaps you have reached that place of "divine desperateness"; perhaps being there is what prompted you to pick up *The Optimystic's Handbook.* If so, isn't it wonderful that all things seem to lead, in some mysterious way, to good—*that your life is happening exactly as it was meant to happen?* As an optimystic, however, you will begin to realize that while pain, disillusionment, restlessness, frustration, grief, despair, and other highly annoying states of being are all valuable doorways to true consciousness, our search for God can also be motivated by a sense of hope and adventure. The optimystic believes that we do not have to be in the throes of misery in order to find our mystic self. In fact, we can begin to make its acquaintance simply by engaging in three painless practices: seeing, appreciating, and releasing.

The Three Steps to Awakening: Seeing, Appreciating, Releasing

Seeing

Just as we think we are awake in life when we are really asleep, so we think we are seeing when we are actually blind to the real wonders around us. The process of awakening involves seeing with new eyes. Look around you now. See things with new eyes, the eyes of someone who has just entered the room for the first time. Now imagine yours are the eyes of someone who has just entered the world—a newborn baby, perhaps, or an alien from another planet. As you see with new eyes, you experience a new life. This is a "baptism," being cleansed of the old, initiated into the new. Baptize yourself in the name of your newly discovered mystic self. You might even want to honor this mystic self with a name.

Mysticism involves a celebration of the ordinary as extraordinary. With your new eyes, look around you at the ordinary things you have taken for granted, and marvel at their extraordinariness. The chair across from you—the mind that designed it, the hands that crafted it, the wood from which it was fashioned, the tree from which the wood came, the seed that grew into the tree, the wind that carried the seed. See the interconnectedness of all things, the great plan of which you are an integral part.

Take some time to think about the difference between looking and seeing. Looking objectivizes and separates; seeing dissolves barriers and allows oneness between viewer and object to occur. As artist and author Frederick Franck observes,

> We do a lot of looking . . . through lenses, telescopes, television tubes . . . but we see less and less. Never has it been more urgent to speak of *seeing*. Ever more gadgets

conspire to take over our thinking, our feeling, our experiencing, our seeing.

What things do you think you see when you may only be looking at them? What things do you prefer to look at but not see? Take time to write down some of these.

Remember that the mystic self has unlimited vision. As we saw in chapter 1, the word *vision* has many meanings: to see not only the present but the future, to experience other dimensions of reality, to have a dream or a higher quest. What if there were a Lenscrafters for the soul, where instead of optometrists we had optomysticists, fitting us with glasses that could give us perfect sight and insight into all the wonders of the universe? Acquiring twenty-twenty optimystic vision means that you are able to see beyond the confines of this "reality" into the limitless realms of possibility.

Practice expanding your vision, looking beyond what is and into what could be. Do you have dreams, goals, a higher purpose or vision to which you would like to direct your energy? What fears could be holding you back? What beliefs might be "blinding" you to the truth, to your mystic power? Would you like to be able to "see into" a confusing situation, to develop more "in-sight"? As you open your inner eyes, open your heart as well. Let all boundaries to your limited vision slowly dissolve. Imagine possibilities becoming reality, dreams coming true.

As you begin to see the world through the eyes of your mystic self, you will find that your perspective on life is dramatically altered. Move away from your own little world into the realm of pure consciousness, where anything is possible and everything that you do or don't do affects the world in ways you might never before have imagined. You can now "envision" with unmistakable clarity. You will become an optimystic visionary, setting goals that your new, limitless vision will help you to achieve, while at the same time paying attention to the importance of combining your actions with higher goals.

Appreciating

Your mystic self appreciates everything about life, even the bad things. Take a moment now to appreciate everything you can think of. Appreciate the very fact that you are alive, that you are breathing, that you have been given this life, that you have an eternal spirit that is being given expression through your body. Appreciate the roof over your head, the work that you are able to do, the talents you have been given, the possessions you have worked for and enjoy. Appreciate the people in your life who are dear to you, who love you and stand by you. Make a list now of everything that you can think of to appreciate, including the negative events that may have led or are leading to positive things you might not have had if they hadn't been given to you. See everything you have now, at this moment—possessions, abilities, job, relationships, circumstances—as gifts, and accept these gifts willingly. If some are harder to accept than others, make a note of these and reflect upon why. Don't judge yourself at this time; if resistance comes up, allow it to speak its piece.

Releasing

Okay. Now that you can appreciate all that has been given to you, let it go. Release it. Give it back to the universe.

Welcome to the world of optimystic paradox. This is a world, you will soon find, in which paradox stretches its legs, lies back, and rests quite comfortably. A world in which seemingly opposing experiences can exist simultaneously at any given moment. As an optimystic, you may find yourself experiencing pain and joy simultaneously or planning for the future while living fully in the moment or letting go, with understanding, hope, and anticipation, of the person or thing that has meant the most to you. When you have reached this stage of optimystic paradox, you will know that you have successfully integrated your physical and metaphysical, material and spiritual selves. For as optimystics, we find that we exist in these two forms and may move back and forth between them at any time.

Practice, for the moment, letting go of everything—ideas, thoughts, experiences, hopes, plans, loves . . . everything. Think about the things that define you, by which you have defined yourself. What would happen if you let these things go, if they left your life? Your mystic self understands the precariousness of an existence based on external measures of definition. Try accepting, just for one moment, the "constant changefulness" of life, as Krishnamurti put it. Realize, just for this moment, that *there are no absolutes*. To awaken to your mystic self is to be completely open to change, transformation, newness. Your mystic self knows that nothing is as it was or as it will be. We may think that experience and knowledge are our anchors, but in reality they may be our chains.

Slowly, let go of your self. Release yourself from your physical body. Experience more of the paradox: we are not our physical body, and yet we must care for this body that has been loaned to us. Like a car that we lease, it must have the best possible care so that we don't have to pay extra charges at the end. As we let go of our attachment to and identification with our physical self, we are required, at the same time, to treat it lovingly, tenderly, appreciatively. Think now about the paradox *of nurturing the self that you are releasing*.

Releasing our attachment to life is the most difficult of all undertakings. Yet it is essential if we are going to be able to fully experience life, to become fully awake and alive. For without attachment we are free, and when we are free we are without fear, and when we are without fear, we are able to truly live.

The Difference Between Releasing and Rejecting

In the West, we often equate mysticism with a rejection of the temporal life. In Western thinking, mystics are often fringe beings, at the very best eccentric, at the very worst highly committable. They walk around in loincloths or sackcloth, eat locusts instead of Big Macs, sit on posts in the middle of the desert for forty years, or retreat into monasteries or ashrams, where they contemplate everything from their navels to their own coffins.

But it is high time we did away with antiquated notions of mysticism as equivalent to asceticism, isolationism, self-purgation, escapism, even eccentricity and insanity. Mysticism is fueled not by the negative energy of rejection (closing the door in fear) but by the positive energy of releasing (opening the door to let something greater in). True mysticism is distinctly, proudly human; it embraces life and the life force through a celebration of the senses.

As you awaken to your inner mystic, you will find yourself seeing things more clearly, from more in-depth and expanded perspectives, and appreciating life more intensely, with the passion of the spirit. Your goal as an optimystic is not to reject the beauty of life, but to embrace and enhance it. We make a mistake when we prevent ourselves from becoming attached to things or people because at some point we are sure to lose them and so think it better—that is, safer—to remain above the "trappings" of life. Life isn't a trap; it's a trip! As optimystics, we urge ourselves to appreciate life's gifts wholly and fully; at the same time, we allow ourselves to release something or someone when the time comes, knowing that this release can only open us up to a greater, newer experience. For this is at the core of the mystic's quest: to make life as rich an *experience* as possible, so that when we pass on, as the Hasidim maintained, we can know paradise when we see it. Why? Because we've already known it on Earth.

3

Sit Down, Shut Up, Open Up

*Where does one find God? In the mountains, the solitary
wooded valleys, strange islands . . . silent music.*

St. John of the Cross

Becoming an optimystic involves finding the quiet time and space
that allows our spirits to speak clearly to us and learning techniques
that lead us into communion with our mystic selves. In many cultures and religions, three of these techniques have been used to
quiet the mind and bring us closer to our essential optimystic
nature. You've undoubtedly heard them referred to as meditation,
contemplation, and centering. These three activities are often confused or used interchangeably, but they are actually separate and
distinct means of achieving the same end. All three help to lead us
to acquire a sense of peace, calmness, and oneness with the self
and the Greater Self of which everything is an eternal, ongoing part.

Meditation is a process of achieving a state of no-thought, complete release of thought. In meditation, one strives to let go of
thoughts, worries, fears, needs—to simply be, until the sense of
moving beyond the physical self and becoming part of a vast land-
scape of awareness is achieved. Contemplation differs from meditation in that it is a *reflective* state. It uses the same tools—silence
and centering—to quiet the mind, but in contemplation one is
reflecting upon an issue or concept in order to gain deeper insight

into it. Centering is a tool that helps us go into meditative and con-templative states. In centering we begin to calm and balance our-selves, to connect with our center, our unchanging core of inner peace. There are many different ways to center oneself. You can say a mantra or prayer, focus on an object such as a candle, walk in slow, measured rhythm, sit at the ocean and let your breathing be-come one with the rising and falling of the waves. Centering is often equated with meditation and contemplation, but it is more accurate to think of it as a focusing device that frees the mind to move into those deeper states of consciousness.

Centering, contemplation, and meditation all teach us how to sit down, shut up, and open up. We sit in a relaxed position that al-lows the energy and breath to move freely through our bodies, both grounding us and opening our receptive channels. We become quiet so that we can hear the heart speak. In the process we open up to what God is really trying to tell us.

Going into a meditative or contemplative state is rather like tak-ing a spiritual bath. We are cleansed of negativity and mental ob-stacles that stand in the way of our contentment. We become more comfortable with exactly who we are as well as who we aren't. We become more peaceful, less affected by stress, more generally de-lightful to be around. One of the most important goals of the opti-mystic is to raise the spirits of others and to make the environment vibrate with peace and hope. But we can't accomplish this if we aren't tuned in to peace and hope ourselves. Meditation and cen-tering practices tune us in; they put us in harmony with the *silent music* that all the elements of the earth play in unison, as a sym-phony of souls. Meditation, contemplation, and centering do not take us away from the Earth; on the contrary, they make us feel part of the Earth on a stronger, deeper level than we ever would have ex-perienced otherwise.

Meditation: Discipline or Good Time?

Meditation, contemplation, and centering have traditionally been viewed as disciplines. Already that word gives them a sobering connotation, like hanging a sign on them that reads "Approach with Caution." Disciplines, after all, are work. They require, quite simply, discipline. And discipline calls to mind intimidating things—homework, exercise, practicing the piano, Sunday school, West Point. . . . Whatever the word *discipline* brings up for you, it probably means, at some basic level, discomfort if not downright suffering.

The very idea of discipline becomes exhausting because we immediately relate it to work and difficulty. Discipline is mountain climbing, not couch potatoing. Discipline is cod liver oil, not banana splits. Discipline is punishment, not reward.

But the truth is that discipline is not in and of itself negative. It is merely a form of training; it helps us develop expertise so that we become good enough at something to genuinely enjoy it. It is our *attitude* toward discipline that determines whether or not the training will be a painful or happy experience. We can look at discipline as a liberating force, one that frees us to expand our talents and our potential so that we can get more out of life; in this light discipline takes on a whole new meaning. And, as optimystics, we can move into the realm of disciplining ourselves to have fun and take life lightly. At this stage discipline really goes through a transformation.

Yes, being happy takes some discipline. It may be hard for us at first to consciously make room for joy in our lives. We are programmed to regard things like fun and play as luxuries to be indulged in only after we've gotten the "real" business of living out of the way. But the optimystic knows that enjoying life is not a luxury but an essential. When we really enjoy life, we're living. When we get into the humor of daily living, we become fully human. We get healthier, our work and relationships improve, and we move that much closer to God—our realized self.

Because its end result is the achieving of inner peace, meditation is merely a doorway to happiness. Nothing more and nothing less. There is no need to view it with the trepidation we feel when we think about going to the gym and sweating ourselves to death in order to finally achieve the perfect body. "I *should* work out today. . . . I *should* go on a low-fat diet. . . . I *should* meditate." Get rid of the notion right now that finding peace and joy in your life is a "should," one more item on a long checklist of things that you ought to be doing and will therefore in all probability never get around to. The experience of peace and joy is your inalienable birthright. You were born with it. It can never be taken away, and all you have to do is discover it, not achieve it. Meditation simply helps you do just that.

So, first of all, we'd like you to view the process of quieting the mind not as discipline but as enjoyment. You're probably familiar with the Chinese image of the Laughing Buddha, a rotund, cheerful soul who epitomizes our soul essence, which is joy. He isn't crying or agonizing; he's basically having a good chuckle because he's gotten the joke. And what's the joke? That the harder we *try* to be happy, the harder it gets. And when we stop *trying* and start *being,* we discover that, presto, we're happy!

Meditation is our natural state of being, which means that busyness and distraction and discomfort and fear and worry are distinctly unnatural states. Therefore, in order to meditate, all we have to do is become our natural self, which is really nothing more than sitting down, shutting up, and opening our hearts to the moment.

Assume a restful position, one that feels natural and relaxed. You don't have to sit on the floor in a full lotus position like all the yogis; you can sit in a chair, or, if you're absolutely most comfortable lying down, go for it. Now, quiet down. Take some deep breaths and relax. Listen to your breathing. Is it rapid? Shallow? Inhale slowly, exhale slowly. Gradually your breath will begin to assume its natural rhythm. Feel it become deeper, calmer. Now, just remain in the present, relaxed, breathing naturally. Let the moment take you where it takes you. If it sounds too simple, it is. Just ten minutes of quiet breathing in and out while letting your mind empty of the day's tension and worry will relax and center you in the moment; not only that, but *the stress-reducing effects of these ten minutes may be felt for as long as several days afterward.*

The question naturally arises as to how many days or months or years one has to meditate before true recognition of our joyous essence takes place. We don't mean to imply that meditation is a one-step, quick-fix process and that all your problems will be solved forever as soon as you do it. Meditating is like any other art; the longer you absorb yourself in it, the better at it you become. If you want to set aside several hours a day for meditation, wonderful. On the other hand, if you can manage only twenty minutes a day, you will still make commendable strides in the direction of a calmer, happier existence. If, as many religious practices suggest, you find the time has come to seek a spiritual guide or master, say the word and one will appear. If eventually you decide to join an ashram or a monastery, we'll be the last ones to stand in your way. Answer the call, whatever it may be. But it is not essential to spend years in arduous practice in order to become a more consistently peaceful and happy person. What we would like to convey here is that connecting to your optimystic nature is not an either/or proposition, in which you either devote yourself to its pursuit twenty-four hours a day or you fail. The reality is just the opposite: *our optimystic nature is our natural state of being.* All we have to do is embrace it and it will embrace us, like two old friends greeting each other with open arms after years of separation.

From Meditating to Optimysticating

There is no question that meditating can be of enormous benefit. But if we start to get hung up on the right way versus the wrong way to meditate, if we start to worry that we're not doing enough or that we're not progressing fast enough, our efforts run the risk of becoming self-defeating. We start trying, instead of simply allowing the process to unfold, and in place of letting go we end up grasping even tighter to our worries, fears, and illusions.

In an effort to help you "un-try" the stubborn knot of meditation expectation, we've coined a new term. Instead of meditating, how about optimysticating?

Optimysticating is, essentially, a *state of exploration designed to help us experience or reexperience the emotions and sensations of joy and hope.* It involves a letting go of all preconceptions and expectations and a letting in of happiness forgotten, despaired of, or as yet undreamed of. Optimysticating may lead us into a state of meditation, or it may not. The important thing is that it leads us toward accepting our optimystic selves and into the mystery itself, without fear or trepidation.

Step One: Finding the Silence

Contemplatives have often referred to silence as the place where God can be heard, which means that silence is not a state of deafness but a state of communion. There is no such thing as true silence, in the sense of absence of noise. Rather, silence is the place we come to in order to truly hear the sound of our own soul. When it is silent around us, the music of the Earth becomes louder; as we said in a previous book, "The world is silent at night so that the moon and the stars can be heard." Just as the Earth has a sacred daily time of rest, quiet, and reflection, in which nature can be listened to and marveled at without the noise and activity that characterize the more boisterous daylight hours, so we need to incorporate regular spaces of quiet into our lives so that we can become more attuned to the heartbeat of the universe.

It's important at first to understand the nature and importance of silence and to create a block of silent time in which to do your optimysticating. Unfortunately, because our society tends to confuse silence with either deafness or emptiness, we are continually tempted to bolt from the quiet, killing any peaceful moments we might find in the day with all manner of noise and distraction.

We must remember that silence invites us to listen to the inner voices that often get ignored or drowned out by the more insistent demands of daily living. Silence acquaints us with ourselves; when we make the time to be quiet and still, we are often surprised by what we find out about who we thought we were. We may encounter aspects of our personality of which we were unaware; we may be astonished to find that within us lives a deeper, wiser being than we had ever suspected. Silence calms us down, helping us to reflect more clearly and to make better decisions. A regular fill-up of quiet time is a good idea, for silence is the fuel that keeps the spirit running smoothly.

In order to get the full benefit of optimysticating, set aside a quiet time and place. A room in your house, a spot in the garden, a rock by a stream—anything will do, as long as you make it your special silent space. When you have created this space, sit in it for a while and simply allow yourself to bask in the comforting warmth of the stillness. Let yourself really hear the silence—the ticking clock, the chirping birds, the crickets, the rustle of leaves, the beating of your heart. Realize what sound really is, what it really means, how, exactly, it resonates in the universe and in you.

Step Two: Finding Your Center

Centering is the oil can that keeps our optimysticating self well lubricated. We'd like to share with you what is probably centering at its simplest, as it was taught to us in Pasadena by a young Buddhist monk, Tokden Rinpoche.

The method is known as Shamata, and the intention is simply to arrive at a calm state of being. Notice that the goal is not to enter into a state of ecstasy or to be rewarded with the thunderclap of enlightenment, only to achieve a restful state of mind. In your a quiet space, sit or lie comfortably. You may close your eyes, although Shamata practitioners suggest keeping them slightly open and focused on a centering object or spot. Now, inhale positive energy and blessings. As you exhale, release your tensions, stresses, and negative emotions. Just let all these things go. Do this three times.

Remain focused on your outgoing and incoming breathing. Whenever thoughts arise, just notice them, let them pass by, and come back to your breathing.

As you become calm, bring your attention to this sense of calmness and rest in it. Become like an innocent child, without judgment or presuppositions. Don't think or visualize; just feel yourself being this wide-eyed, openhearted child.

There is no reason to react to your thoughts, either to become attached to them or to repress them. Just let them go as waves come and go in the ocean, knowing that your nature mind, like the ocean bottom, is still and that, like the waves that dissolve back into the sea, all thoughts will eventually disappear into the stillness of the mind.

Keep coming back to the sense of calmness. If you have become distracted by a thought or emotion, just return and reconnect to the calm abiding. Effortlessly relax.

Do this for as long as you like. A minimum of ten minutes is suggested; you'll probably find that you want to do it for a longer period just because it feels so good. When you are ready to end your session, repeat the first step of inhaling positive energy and blessings and exhaling tension and stress three times. Then open your eyes fully and return to the world refreshed.

During the demonstration, Tokden Rinpoche reminded us that consistency is essential. Even five minutes of Shamata breathing in the morning and evening, he assured us, will change our life. We will be able to release anger, resentments, and fears, to notice them when they arise and to let them go. This freedom from negative emotions will not happen instantly, but with consistency it *will* happen. And as we become calm, so the effects of our calmness will be felt by others.

Step Three: Finding Joy

Now that you've sat down and shut up, it's time to open up. In your silent space, notice your thoughts and feelings, especially where you might be feeling tension in your body. Don't try to do anything. Don't even try not to try! Just be. If you feel tension, exhale it. Imagine any tense parts of your body going limp, heavy, completely surrendered as you release them from the grip of stress and fear.

Now, begin to remember how joy feels. What, to you, are the components of this state that we call joy? What sort of physical and emotional sensations does it produce? When have you felt joy in your life? When you fell in love? When you took your first trip to Disneyland? When you had a child? Whatever memory reawakens the sensation of joy in you, sit with it. Become it. Put yourself back into it, into that moment, until you are actually physically reexperiencing the sensations of joy—the lightness of being, the dizzy, electric energy, the soaring, boundless happiness, the feeling of your heart breaking open with thankfulness. If your heart is broken, use this feeling of joy as grout to fill the cracks. Breathe it into yourself, especially into those areas of your body in which you felt or still feel any tension. Replace the tightness of tension with the lightness of joy.

You will find, as you do this more and more, that joy, at its most basic level, is really a sense of freedom. When we are in joy, we feel released from fear and worry. We are happy with ourselves; we feel free to be who we are, without fear of ridicule or rejection. When we are joyful, we feel more inclined toward curiosity, we are more able to explore the unknown and to take risks because we feel more energetic and more trusting of people, life, and ourselves. Our spirit can speak to us more clearly when we are not drowning it out with the high-decibel chatter of fear and suspicion; the more joyous we are, the more faith we have in our creative power to overcome obstacles and find meaning in life's challenges.

It is this sense of freedom that lies at the heart of optimysticism—a freedom not of the body but of the spirit. As we become more centered, as we meditate, contemplate, and optimysticate more regularly, we become aware that freedom is a natural state of being, for our minds and our spirits always have the freedom to roam the universe, to contact many levels of knowledge and information beyond that which can be processed only by the intellect or the physical self. No longer do we have to blame our circumstances for our unhappiness, for any lack of fulfillment in our lives. Our spirit is not impressed by physical limitations; it knows that it has the power to pass through any wall of fear our mind has erected to keep us from feeling joy.

So, as you are fully *enjoying* your feeling of joy, realize that it is not a past phenomenon, a lost moment. It is here with you now; it is a part of you that you can contact at any time. It is your optimystic self, your natural state of being. Optimysticate now on this happy discovery. Be "in joy"—enjoy!

4

Is There Life *Before* Death?

We are all searching for an experience of being alive, more so than looking for meaning.

JOSEPH CAMPBELL

It is natural to ponder the question "Is there life after death?" An optimystic, however, is more concerned with whether there will be an experience of life and aliveness *before* death. To take it a step further, we ask ourselves if we are as alive as we possibly can be.

Everyone experiences being alive, regardless of how little or how much they participate in the experience. Yet the optimystic seeks a deeper experience of aliveness, one in which he or she is taking part in the mystery, participating with full awareness, exploring the full range of exhilarating possibilities that this physical adventure offers.

Stop here for a moment to reflect on how alive you feel right now. Take a pen and paper and write down your answers to the following questions: How do you tend to respond to life? Are you an active participant? A passive one? Do you pursue activities that give you joy, or does life seem to be passing you by? Do you often allow yourself the experience of full, unbridled happiness? Do you live in the now or in the yesterday or the tomorrow? What are the things that make you feel madly, truly, deeply alive?

From early childhood, many of us have been conditioned to suppress our natural urge toward joy. We learn how to inhibit our impulses so as to be more socially acceptable. We don't laugh too loud; we stifle our tears. We do what gets us approval, to the point where the dividing line between what we really want and what others want for us becomes severely blurred. As we move toward what we are told will reward us with success, ignoring the needs of our spirits and souls, we probably will find, sooner or later, the paradox of the full bank account and the empty life.

Optimysticism is a twofold path, involving an active belief in life in and beyond the physical. One of the most rewarding things about becoming optimystic is the discovery of who we are and what we value on the deepest level. In the process we begin to discover what it feels like to be truly alive, both physically and spiritually. When our physical and spiritual selves are well integrated, when we feel at peace in both our bodies and our souls, we are able to experience life on the most exciting and profound levels of awareness.

It is important that you find your own way to have an authentic experience of living in your body. We may suggest that you drop everything and run outside to jump for joy at the sight of an incredible sunrise, but we also understand that you may not be the exuberant type. This is okay. Some optimystics find working quietly on a model airplane a genuinely exhilarating life experience. Other optimystics break out into songs and dance spontaneously, not caring a wink for what others may think. Some optimystics find it very easy to tell people how much they care for them; others hide their feelings, sneaking them out in simple, unexpected expressions of love. There is no better time to start experiencing life than right now, but you must experience *your* life, not the life you feel others expect you to live. You must have your authentic experience.

In order to do this, begin by noticing what you are drawn to and why. Also notice what you try to talk yourself out of. When do you use your intellect, your rational self, as a defense against the messages your heart and soul might be trying to get through to you? Do you feel unfulfilled or incomplete in any areas of your life? Are you afraid to look at what might make you feel really alive because of the change, the risk, it might involve? Are you surviving or thriving?

Revering Life

To get past surviving mode and enter thriving mode, the optimystic must acquire reverence for the eternal mystery and wonder of life. Reverence allows us to connect deeply with what it really means to be here on Earth, to respect the divine energy that created, and therefore is present in, all things. Our birth represents an agreement we made to be physically present and to experience the passion, pain, love, and greatness that humans are capable of. But above all, the agreement included reverence, which is a response of honoring life on all levels.

One of the most disturbing aspects of today's society is a lack of reverence for the Earth and its inhabitants, as well as a void where the sacred used to be. Ancient practices of ritual and prayer can still serve us well; they can remind us that every breath we take, every action we make, is a gift as well as an opportunity to bring the sacred into our daily existence. Grace at meals, for instance, is probably the most common of these ancient rituals persisting into the present day. Many religions have specific prayers for specific times of day, probably because the human mind is notoriously forgetful and needs to be reminded, every few hours, of the divine presence that permeates every aspect of life. With these structured prayers, people became attuned to the sacredness of all times of day, from the stirrings of the dawn to the full force of the sun in all its splendor to the onset of the night and the peaceful, imperturbable presence of the stars to, once more, the wonder of the new dawn. In the process the day becomes an unconscious metaphor for our own life—being born, flowering, withering, dying, and being resurrected. Through prayer and the incorporation of the sacred into everyday affairs, we learn to move with the rhythms of the universe and to respect them. This makes us a vital link to the past as well as to the future. As the Tibetan teacher Pema Chodron observes,

> Ritual, when it's heartfelt, is like a time capsule. It's as if thousands of years ago, somebody had a clear, unobstructed view of magic, power and sacredness and realized that if he went out each morning and greeted the sun in a very stylized way . . . it connected him to that richness. Therefore he taught his children to do that, and his children taught their children. . . . So thousands of years later, people are still doing it and connecting with the same feeling.

One of the ways we can begin to tune in to our natural capacity for reverence is by bringing a sense of the sacred back into our lives. We can do this by taking time out for moments of reverence. You might want to incorporate a prayer or ritual that appeals to you into your regular activities, setting aside a few minutes at specific times of the day in which to give thanks for and to appreciate the moment or to contemplate the marvels that are always around us. You can take time out to reconnect to the sacred upon awakening, at work, at lunch, or on break, at dinner, before you retire, or whenever seems appropriate to you. You might want to share these moments with your family, a friend, or a co-worker; optimystics enjoy spreading reverence around!

You are also perfectly free to experience moments of reverence that do not have to be part of any formal religious ceremony but instead might involve any daily experience. The following scenarios are common opportunities for reverent responses to life. How do they affect you?

1. Imagine that you are driving down the street and you see two young men with Down's syndrome laughing and eating ice cream. What would your first thought be?

If your first impulse is to feel pity or fear or superiority, try switching from ego mode to reverence mode. Contemplate the fact that every soul has agreed to come into this life and remain here for a reason. A reverent response to this scene would not be pity for someone who is mentally disabled but rather delight in that person's ability to experience his or her own unique joy in life and in the moment.

2. Imagine that a majestic tree in your neighborhood is being cut down in front of your eyes to make room for a shopping mall. What would you do?

A reverent person would feel pain at the sight of a beautiful tree being wantonly destroyed; an *actively* reverent person would try to stop the proceedings if they hadn't gone too far or would become involved in some sort of volunteer environmental protection work to guard against similar desecrations in the future. Realize that reverence is not only an emotion or a response also but a form of activism. There may be times when you are called upon to put your reverence on the line—to channel it into positive action.

3. Imagine walking down a crowded street seeing exquisitely beautiful clouds lit up by the setting sun, casting warm rich colors on the faces of your fellow humans.

Most of us are so busy getting somewhere or are so involved with our thoughts and plans when we're walking along that we forget to look up above "I level." When we are too absorbed in ourselves and our plans, we tend to miss the beauty not only of nature but of other human beings. We're reminded to revere all life, but how can we feel reverence for something we don't even notice? The next time you see someone on the street, try this exercise: Look at that person as you. For one moment, appreciate his or her life, value it as intensely as you do your own. Feel your sense of separateness dissolving; become one with this person. You'll feel a momentary flooding of your being with love, compassion, and reverence. Now, bless this person in any way you like. Send love, good cheer, God's peace. Did you realize, as you blessed this person, that you were also being blessed?

Reverence is an integral aspect of compassion. True reverence is not annulled when we are angry or are facing other difficult emotions. Instead, when we revere life, our anger and sadness will not allow us to hurt others as a response. Too often humans get into attack mode when they are angry and unhappy. We must remember that other people are not here to make us happy or unhappy or to be blamed for anything we are going through. We *are* here to, as Manly P. Hall said, "co-operate and cheat the devil." Lack of reverence on any level of life creates a painful imbalance for the world's soul; where reverence is present, love is given back to life and balance is restored.

Breaking Spells

A spell is an incantational word or formula or a bewitched state or a state of compelling attraction. Spells are different from mere negative messages. We can always choose to accept or reject a negative message. But a spell is a message with power that has somehow taken up residence in our psyche, dictating our behavior on an unconscious level. As such, spells can set up expectations that prevent us from having an authentic moment-to-moment life.

To some extent, all of us are under spells—beliefs that have been ingrained in us and that we hold to for reasons that we've never stopped to think about. Some of the spells people find themselves under may be projections from others, a psychic prediction they have been given, the idea that aging and maturing is negative, or a label from childhood that they have accepted without question and have lived out into adulthood. When we are under a spell, we become caught up in a perception of ourselves or a certain behavior pattern that limits our vision and can cause us to become victims of self-fulfilling prophecies rather than agents of change and renewal.

List any situation you may think of that could qualify as having cast, in some way, a spell over you. Are you living out any predictions made for you when you were a child or living up to expectations placed on you that were not your own? Has there been an authority figure in your life, such as a parent, teacher, lover, spouse, whom you have allowed to determine the state of your sense of self? Do you often act from a "should" rather than a "want" mode?

The word *spell* also originates from the Old English word for story. A story holds powerful energy, and, fortunately, a story can be retold and rewritten. Freeing ourselves of spells means rewriting our stories. This process can take more effort than we realize, because we first must do some inner work to examine the effect that stories have on us. We must discover the story living in our psyche that someone else has put there before we can rewrite it. We may choose to actually write the story on paper, then edit and change it. We can speak it into a tape recorder, then retell it. If you are living a story that is not optimystic, your first task is to become aware of it. Awareness always alters the situation or issue.

Here is a storytelling exercise that you can do to achieve more clarity on your current state of aliveness.

1. Write the story of your life in a few succinct paragraphs. What are the outstanding features of it? Describe your personality. Are there patterns in your life that seem to repeat themselves? Who were some of your important role models and influences? What character traits and spiritual values have helped or hindered you in your life?

2. Would you like to rewrite this story in any way? Do so now if you feel like it.

3. What course would you like the rest of your life to take? Write down how you'd like to envision your future. *You're* the storyteller; be bold, be fascinating. See if you can enthrall yourself with your own story.

After you have written the final statement on the issue, turn it over to the Great Creator with a little prayer, trusting that the highest good will always prevail. Set it aside, along with any worry, self-judgment, or self-criticism that may have held you back in the past. Allow yourself, from this moment on, to be open to the new self that is always emerging.

The Spell of Fear of Dying

It is easy to scare ourselves to death these days. Anyone who watches the local news is exposed to a body count of the day's treacherous deaths. Like ghouls prowling the graveyards in search of excitement, our newscasters delight in sensationalizing scenes

and stories involving dead bodies. As a result, we become convinced that death is just around our own corner, and we turn our
energy toward doing everything in our power to lessen our chances
of experiencing it. Thanks to our built-in survival instinct, fear of
death is a given. But the optimystic asks, might fear of death also be
a given in the sense of a gift—an opportunity to look directly into
the fear and out again? As fears are so often the seeds from which
enlightenment springs, might our great fear of death be the opportunity we've secretly been looking for to laugh fear out of our lives
and concentrate on *living?*

To what degree is fear choking the life out of you? Some people
become daredevils to avoid letting fear rule them. Others hide
away, manifesting experiences of fear in their minds that slowly kill
them. We have to respect our individual temperaments, but we also
must agree that too much fear of death means too little sacred experience. Knowing that death is a part of life is not just a cliché; it
is an eternal truth. Accepting the fear of death enables us to begin
to make peace with death as a natural aspect of our humanness.
While fear of death can make us depressed, it is actually something
meant to keep us alive and *out of* depression. It is the mirror side of
our survival instinct; we fear death because we want life. The question is, how can we break free of fear in order to live more fully,
more authentically?

If you find that you're afraid of living, on some level, because
you're so afraid of dying, you might want to think of some ways to
use the powerful energy of your fear in order to break its spell over
you. After all, energy is energy. Whether it comes from fear or from
joy, it exists as a force for change. Try the following technique,
which is used in Gestalt therapy to awaken us to the many different
sides of our psyche that demand attention. See your fear not as separate from you but as part of you. That means that you *are* your fear.
Become it; speak in its voice; write down what it has to tell you.
Now, trade places and talk to your fear. Tell it how you feel about it
and what it is doing to you. Have a dialogue with it, and make sure
you record the conversation in some way, either on tape or in writ-

ing immediately afterward. Do not be afraid of any deep emotions, such as sadness or anger, that might unexpectedly surface. Allow them to be expressed. Cry, yell, let it out. This is the actual physical energy of fear; use it. Give it a voice and channel it straight through you and out of you.

After such dialogues, it is not uncommon to feel a sense of a great burden being lifted, a surge of energy, a sensation of tremendous lightness or joy. What a wonderful step toward living!

Becoming an Explorer of Life

We're all familiar with know-it-alls and how annoying they can be. Who wants to be around someone who has all the answers and never lets you forget it? But ultimately the reason we can't stand know-it-alls is not because they're obnoxious but because they're boring and they live boring lives. They aren't good at listening because they already know the answer. They aren't good at appreciating because they're not open to new experience. They aren't good at empathizing because they "told you so." The know-it-all hates spontaneity; in his desperate need to believe that life is reassuringly predictable, he has a great need to keep a choke hold on his environment. Sadly, his knowledge becomes not his joy but his prison.

Optimystics, on the other hand, approach life in the spirit of discovery. The optimystic enjoys the *process* of life and is not put off by the discomfort of the unknown. We are here to learn. That's what wisdom is all about—learning on our own, discovering for ourselves. That's why things get hard or frustrating—so that we can acquire wisdom through suffering, faith through wisdom, and peace through faith. Remember that God likes us to work a little, to look, question, wonder, uncover. What fun would a treasure hunt be if the treasure were set out in broad daylight, right under our noses, with a big sign saying, "Treasure Here"?

The university of life is in session around the clock. But, unlike our standard universities, which grade us on what we know or seem to know, this higher school of learning gives us As for what we don't know and are not afraid to admit we don't know. Optimystics don't define themselves by the degree of their ability to reel off facts or give answers and solutions. This is the ego realm, not the realm of the mystic self. Our mystic selves are far better listeners than pontificators. As the mystic is happily ensconced in the "cloud of unknowing," in which the limited and often false perceptions of mind knowledge are replaced by the unlimited awareness of soul knowledge, so the optimystic is open to the many possibilities that life offers for growth and prefers to explore rather than prejudge them.

Optimystic reverence for life keeps us open to the beauty of the moment, which is where life begins. The Jewish philosopher Abraham Heschel defined this special kind of reverence as "radical amazement"—a feeling of profound appreciation for the magnificence of our creation, our very existence. To be radically amazed by life is to be continually open to its delights and surprises. This is when we are truly alive—when we shed our fears, preconceptions, and illusions long enough to simply *be* in the present moment, the present experience, not just as an observer but as a participant. Immersing ourselves in life so deeply that we move out of our limited notion of self to "become the moment" and trust it enough to lead us where it will is the mark of the true explorer of life.

Here's a good becoming-the-moment exercise. Stop here and just be still. Rein in your mind; cease, for one minute, analyzing, criticizing, worrying, indulging in either memory or daydreaming. Simply experience the moment, *not as your self but as the moment*. Let things be completely as they are. (Where are they?) Think of yourself as a transparent energy field of Divine consciousness. What sounds seem to pass through you? Keep your eyes open and don't focus, let things blur. . . . Have you gone anywhere? Has the moment taken you away, or given you a more solid presence? To end the exercise, take a deep breath and center yourself.

When we do this exercise we begin to get an inkling of what it feels like to be one with everything. We take the first baby step toward moving outside of ourselves; we begin to experience what it really means to be more than our bodies; we glimpse how our thoughts, preconceptions, and expectations obscure what is and what therefore could be. And we get an idea of how precious, how valuable this moment is—especially if it were to be our last.

As an explorer of life, the optimystic knows that he or she is also a creator of life. As such, responsibility can be taken in the moment. If, as optimystics, we are aware of our unity with all things, we are also aware that how we choose to react or respond to a situation naturally affects the very atmosphere we share with other humans. If we're standing in a never-ending line at the Department of Motor Vehicles, we can choose to add to the stress of the atmosphere by becoming angry and impatient. Or we can choose to make things calmer by being friendly and cheerful or by using the waiting time to meditate. However we decide to respond to the moment, we do have an effect.

The great spiritual teacher Krishnamurti spent his entire lifetime exploring the depth of the moment and showing others how being fully in that moment, and nowhere else, awakens us to a constantly shifting, new reality. This is the experience of living, as closely as possible, in the state of pure awareness that comes with putting on not a new pair of glasses but a new pair of eyes. He wrote in his journals,

> Early this morning, there was a benediction that seemed
> to cover the earth and fill the room. . . . Every time there
> is something "new" in this benediction, a "new" quality, a
> "new" perfume, but yet it is changeless. It is utterly un-
> knowable.

Krishnamurti was an expert on life before death. He lived in a state of radical amazement, alert at all times to the beauty and power of the moment. This is all the more astonishing considering the fact that he suffered from intense headaches from the age of twenty-eight until his death at ninety-four. No cure was ever found for this chronic affliction, so Krishnamurti decided to treat it as just another opportunity to experience the mystery of living. He referred to the pain not in terms of its physical misery, but merely as "the process."

> The process was particularly intense yesterday afternoon
> . . . almost unbearable . . . Whereupon the room became
> full with that benediction. . . . It was the centre of all cre-
> ation; it was a purifying seriousness.
> (*The Notebooks of Krishnamurti*)

This is the ultimate achievement of the truly alive person—to be able to see suffering as a new and meaningful experience so that it is no longer suffering, just the "process" of living.

If we can learn anything from Krishnamurti, it is that "freedom is the emptying of the mind of experience." In other words, real freedom consists in liberating ourselves from all forms of attachment, including thoughts based on previous experience. For previous experience often conditions us to expect things to be a certain way rather than to be fully open to new possibilities. We all know the New Age catch phrase, "Expect a miracle." Krishnamurti would say instead, "Expect nothing, but be open to anything."

And so the optimystic, walking through the open door of the moment into new worlds, truly understands the Taoist saying, "Cease expecting, and you gain all things."

5

What's So Great About Security?

Give up everything for God.

You say that, and you don't know what you mean.

In the Cathedral at Louisville, the afternoon I came here, I knew: it meant going by the way you know not, to get what you can't know. Every time you forget that, and every time you think you know where you are going, you are no longer living for God alone, for we only go to Him in darkness of self-denial, by the way we do not know.

THOMAS MERTON

In 1942, Thomas Merton wrote the above reflection in his journals detailing his experiences in the monastic life. When you think about Merton, the worldly Eastern intellectual, getting a call one day to serve God and ending up a Catholic monk in an abbey in the hills of Kentucky, you realize how little we really know about life—how much of what happens to us is totally unpredictable, impossible to plan for. And you realize that when we try too hard to predict, plan, and control our destiny—when we rely too much on our belief in and need for what we call security—we risk missing the once-in-a-lifetime chance to reach our true measure as human beings and beings of God.

Most of us spend a large part of our lives running after what we perceive of as security. We believe that a good job, a good marriage or relationship, a nice house, or a hefty savings account will protect us against adversity forever. In other words, most of us live in the realm of illusion. None of these things is real, in the sense of being permanent. The only thing that is real is loss. But being human and keyed up for physical survival, we prefer not to think about the inevitability of loss. Instead, we continually plan for and live in the future, as if we had one whit of control over it. And in the process we live in a state of grasping onto things that we feel will secure that future and in fear that these things might be taken from us.

Unlike your average everyday human, the optimystic does not fear that the trappings of security might someday be taken; he or she *knows* that they certainly will be. And unlike your average everyday human, the optimystic therefore asks, not, "How can I find security?" but "What's so great about security?" What's so great about having an orderly, predictable, comfortable, "controllable" existence? As optimystics, we understand that in letting go of preconceptions about security, we are that much freer to live more intensely, more passionately, more soul-fully.

An Optimystic Knows That Life Is Risky Business

Risk is the possibility of harm or loss and exposure to a chance of loss or damage. Because as humans we're conditioned to survive, we tend to equate taking risks with living on the edge. And this, we're told, is foolish. Don't take risks. Stay in your job, however much you hate it. Stay in your relationship, however bored you've become. Keep the status quo, don't play the stock market, and, for heaven's sake, don't follow your dreams, which are the biggest risks of all!

Yet we yearn to risk—to live boldly, to realize our visions, to be active, not passive, participants in life. Have you ever thought about the themes that pervade movies and literature, our two most potent means of cathartic living? Every movie and every novel you've ever read revolves, on some level, around the theme of risk—either risks taken that changed lives or risks not taken that were forever regretted.

The optimystic knows that *to risk is to live*. He or she also knows that, contrary to our security fantasies, life is, by its very nature, a continual risk. We are always living on the edge—either the edge of self-discovery or the edge of death. To deny this is to deny ourselves the chance to really experience the multidimensional nature of our earthly existence.

In 1933, British novelist I. A. R. Wylie wrote:

> Either life is a tremendous adventure or it is nothing. And it is only when we behave and "feel" ourselves as adventurers, who have cast away safety, that we become invulnerable. . . . We must accept the fact that danger and uncertainty are really the breath of life. We must admit that we undermine ourselves by our demand for a safety and permanence that really bores us to death. Mentally and spiritually, we must strip ourselves of the deadly obesity which comes of habit and security. . . . What we have to realize ourselves, and teach the next generations, is that only through fearless acceptance of change and a stern preparation of our souls and bodies to meet it can we hope to come through with our real treasure intact. ("The Challenge of Change," *Readers Digest*)

As optimystics, we cannot afford to fear change. Instead, we need to look at change as creative energy simply waiting to be used. Nothing, after all, is stationary. Even if it isn't visible to the naked eye, change is occurring every instant, from shifts in particles, atomic structure, and energy to shifts in perception and consciousness. Add to this the fact that no two people see any one thing exactly alike because we all view the world through the unique filter of our own personal experience. Change is life, and risk is adaptation to change. Therefore, to take risks and to greet insecurity with hope rather than fear are crucial steps in the direction of moving from surviving to thriving.

Risk is a force of energy that holds great promise. We take risks because they inevitably lead us onward. But optimystics take risks wisely in order to proceed upward. Many of us are so afraid of taking risks that we downscale, leading truncated, unfulfilled, but predictable lives. Others take unwise risks, devoid of foresight or strategy, and so experience a continual pattern of frustration and difficulty. As optimystics, we need to be able to discern the difference between a life-affirming and a life-destroying risk. We need to know when to forge ahead, when to stay still, when to retreat. Life has its little and big ups and downs. It is like a roller-coaster or an enchanted ride into the tunnel of love—the optimystic amusement park, full of thrills, packed to the gills with the unexpected, yet always bringing us, sooner or later, safely home. The one thing we don't want is to know too much about what is ahead of us. This is why optimystics usually like the hills and dales rather than the flat view of the prairie. Both hold beauty, but one encourages the excitement of surprise and discovery.

The Optimystic Knows That Life Is Out of Control

In our technologically alienated age, we live in the complete illusion of control, choosing to disregard the fact that in actuality we live in a continual state of uncertainty. We persist in the belief that loss of security happens to other people, not us—except when it does happen to us and we find ourselves completely unprepared for it. The optimystic, on the other hand, lives comfortably with uncertainty. As the Boy Scout's motto is "Be prepared," so the optimystic's motto is "Be prepared—for loss of control." This does not mean helplessness or victimization, however. The optimystic knows that *we can't control life; we can only control our attitude toward life*.

Indigenous people and other cultures are far more evolved in their understanding of how little control we have over anything. But modern technology finds idol or fetish worship or clearly defined ritual immensely amusing. Who but simpletons would give over their own power to an inert object? But in truth what such forms of worship say is, "I realize that I don't have control over my environment, that the danger of loss is ever present. Therefore, I surrender to the superior wisdom of a higher power and to my own strength as a flexible human being to bend in whatever direction the fates stretch me." The Catholic worship of saints, along with veneration of crucifixes, statues of the Virgin, miraculous medals, and relics, is a form of this spiritual letting go. All of our religions understand that prayer, ritual, and objects that link us to the divine are all healthy forms of surrender.

And in technosociety, don't we have our own form of idol worship? Look at our dependence on computers. We rely on them for everything. When they go down we're helpless until a computer consultant—the high priest of technoreligion—can come to our rescue and intercede. We feel so all-powerful manipulating this machine to perform all sorts of miracles; we surf the Net with blissful omniscience. But in reality it is the computer that so subtly controls us, making us its slave through dependency.

Like sleepwalkers in a dream of being at the controls, we are unconscious of the fact that we're the ones who are being controlled. We are unaware that because we have become alienated from our spiritual centers and from our environments, we have lost our ability to fend for ourselves. What we really want is spiritual security. But we don't realize that. So, when we encounter a serious upset or loss, when the rug is pulled out from under us, we continue to search for security in the rubble of our shattered illusions about it rather than understanding the limits of our human control and learning to trust in the unexpected.

The Illusions of Security: The Four Confessions

As optimystics, we ultimately have to be honest with ourselves about the bogus nature of security. We have to confess our "sin" of worshiping the god of security before we can become free to follow the lead of the true God within. So, the following are the Four Optimystic Confessions about security:

1. *Security can be boring.* It might make us feel more comfortable to always know where we are headed, to plan for a future that we expect to turn out a certain way, to be in uneventful but predictable relationships. But what we're trading for comfort is passion and excitement. Oh, yeah, we buy those romance novels by the barrel to make up for it. But when all is said and done, wouldn't we prefer to have an actual rather than vicarious experience of the intensity of life? As humans, we tend to distrust the unknown. As optimystics, we move to redefine *the unknown* as *the unexplored.* As explorers of life, optimystics can't afford to be tied to the apron strings of security. This doesn't mean that optimystics can't make money or have successful careers or stable, fulfilling, long-term relationships. It just means that they are willing to take risks, in the spirit of adventure, in order to fully experience the adventure of the spirit.

2. *Security can be a prison in disguise.* We might have a Porsche or a great big house or a $20,000 stereo system. We might have a nice fat pension waiting for us at the end of the retirement rainbow. On the other hand, we might be living simply or getting by on just enough. The question to ask ourselves is, In trying to acquire material security or in just trying to maintain the status quo, are we genuinely happy? To what have we become attached in order to maintain our current lifestyle? Has our work become our prison? Are we chained to our career? Are we stressed, worn out, and headed for a heart attack but terrified to leave for fear of losing our security? And what about our personal life? Are our relationships with our spouse, our children, our friends fulfilling? Do we have enough time and energy to make them so? Are we too busy at the job or business to do the things we really want to do, to be the person we really want to be with those we love? Security has no meaning whatsoever if pursuing it prevents us from living the life we really dream of living, and if it prevents us from realizing our true potential as physical *and* spiritual beings.

3. *Security can be a con artist.* Just when you think you've got it, look out—it's gone. Because life is temporary, anything of the Earth is only on loan to us, including our own bodies. So no

amount of financial security, not even the perfect relationship, can give us security.

You have believed in security, and it has let you down. You have invested so much in the pursuit of security, only to discover that there's no such thing. Now what?

4. *Security can take us away from our real purpose.* It is a siren along the spiritual journey, singing to us from the Prudential Rock, luring us into believing that there is actually such a thing as "life insurance." In search of security, we follow its call instead of the song of our own hearts and souls. We forget what we're here for; we ignore our dreams. And we ignore the call of our mystic selves to become centered in faith, to experience the true security of oneness with the divine, to invest in the only reliable institution left in the world—God's Savings and Loan. In pursuit of a trust, have we forgotten how to trust—in the higher spiritual power that will always rescue us, no matter how dire our circumstances? What greater security can there be than the revelation that we are more than our bodies, more than our physical existence—that we really cannot and do not die, except to our earthly illusions?

The Benefits of Uncertainty

Optimystics know that uncertainty is the prelude to discovery, and discovery is the prelude to growth. In other words, uncertainty can be a real blessing. It can propel us in new directions. It can make us take risks and live more radically, more intensely. Uncertainty can turn us in the direction of our spiritual selves; so often it is a security crisis in our lives that brings us to spiritual awakening and peace. Uncertainty may force us to face our fragility, giving us the opportunity to lay down the burden of our illusions of control—to face life naked but free, open to a new destiny. We are humbled, more reverent toward a higher power, more appreciative of the things and people that contribute to our sense of well-being. Optimystics believe that God likes to rattle us a little, perhaps because the noise reminds us of his or her presence!

You don't have to live on the edge; that's not what we're saying. We are not advocating feeling insecure in the sense of helpless, grasping, fearful, and inferior. What we are saying is that security is an illusion and that uncertainty is the reality of the human condition. Viewed from this angle, insecurity is actually the opposite of helplessness, grasping, or low self-esteem. It is a state of unsureness and therefore of great openness to any and all possibilities. When you are not secure, you can't hold on, which means you have to let go. As a result, you are no longer shackled to constraining beliefs and fears. Instead, you are free to soar to your higher destination, and things of the spirit are now free to come into your life through the open space you have just created.

The Security of Love

There's a wonderful children's story by English author Eleanor Farjeon entitled "The Kind Farmer." It's about a rich farmer in a small village who's the biggest miser around. He's so afraid to part with an extra penny that his life is one continual experience of fear. He lives in tormented terror of lack, of insecurity. Of course, everyone in the village either hates him or pities him. But one day he meets a beautiful woman with a pure heart who sees the possibilities in his soul. He falls in love with her, marries her, and of course tries to possess her, in fear of losing her. But she dies in childbirth. Now the farmer has a little daughter, upon whom he lavishes all of his love. He's always buying her pretty things, and the first word she associates with him is *kind*. She calls him her "Kind Da," and the stingy, cranky farmer is totally taken aback, as no one has ever used that word in connection with him before. He finds he likes the sound of it so much that he wants to hear it again and again. So he does more nice things for his little girl. And the more he hears her call him "kind," the more desperate he becomes to validate her opinion of him.

It isn't too long before the little girl is convincing him to do kind things for others as well. At first it's tough; parting with a penny or two for a beggar is as painful as losing a tooth. But his daughter's response—"Kind Da!"—is the best painkiller around. The farmer begins doing more and more for the poor and needy in the village, until he is actually unable to stop. Continually hungry for his little girl's approval, he begins to be motivated by her joy and the joy of those he is helping. And eventually he becomes the most earnest philanthropist the town has ever known. As the years go by, he becomes poorer and poorer, giving all his money away. Finally, one day, he is found dead, without a penny to his name. But the entire town rises to the occasion, taking in his child and lavishing everything upon her. His legendary kindness has become an eternal flame of love and protection, ensuring his daughter's welfare forever.

And the moral of this story—and of similar, more famous fables like *It's a Wonderful Life* and *A Christmas Carol*—is: The degree of true security we experience in our lives is directly proportional to the degree to which we are able to give and receive love. When we allow ourselves to love fully, without condition or obstruction, so much love flows back into our life that we can never for one moment feel really insecure.

We may run out of money, but we can never run out of love. If we run out of money but we have loved as hard and well as we possibly could, chances are we will have a multitude of friends, a great human safety net to break our fall. The optimystic knows that since love is the only real security we have and the greatest gift we can give to anybody, we must, like the kind farmer, never cease dispensing it until it pervades our entire being, our entire life, ruling us, humbling us, ennobling us.

Having Without Clinging

Nonattachment and surrendering don't mean nonenjoyment or even nonacquisition. We can enjoy the comforts of this world, we can desire things to make our lives and environments more pleasant and beautiful, and we can work toward these things. But unless we can have them without clinging to them, without defining our lives by them, we set ourselves up for pain—the pain of the eventual, inevitable loss and emptiness that always accompanies impermanence. For the optimystic it's not "Look but don't touch," but rather, "Touch but don't grasp."

An Exercise in Enjoying and Releasing

Here's an optimystic exercise in both enjoying and releasing, which will help you to appreciate earthly pleasures while at the same time resting secure in the knowledge that these things can at any moment be removed from your life—in order that something new, untried, and equally if not more satisfying may be allowed to enter.

1. Get quiet. Do a minute or two of centering practice as we described in chapter 3.

2. Now, think of an item you really want or are planning to purchase, say, a new software package you've had your eye on or a new sofa. Imagine purchasing the item—how good it feels to finally have it, own it. Imagine using it—stretching out on the sofa, playing with the new software. Feel your enjoyment; get into it. *Optimysticate* on it!

3. When you are really luxuriating in your new acquisition, imagine that it's suddenly taken away. Your dog rips up the sofa. The software has a virus. Ouch, double ouch. Feel the sting of the loss. Let it come into you.

4. Now, let go of any attachment you might have felt toward these items. They're gone. There's nothing you can do. Oh, well. Think of what can now come into your life. An even more comfortable sofa? An updated software package? Realize that none of these items is irreplaceable. Breathe deeply; feel the freedom of nonattachment.

5. Of course, these are minor losses. So let's take the exercise to the next level. Imagine a major purchase you're planning or hoping to make someday. A new car or a new house, for instance. Repeat steps 1 and 2. When you get to step 3, imagine that your car is stolen or your new house burns down. Get into the devastation of the loss. You have no transportation. Everything that was dear to you, from your treasured antiques to family photos, is gone forever. Spend a few minutes with whatever feelings arise. Fear, terror, rage, desperation, grief . . . Experience these feelings as deeply, as realistically, as you can.

6. Now let it all go. All the fear, all the attachment. It is safe to do this because this devastating loss hasn't happened in reality, only in your imagination. Let go of the car, the house. Breathe in blessings, breathe out the rage, sadness, and fear. Feel, in this moment, the supreme gift of your aliveness. Can you hear your heartbeat? Feel the blood coursing through your veins? Take a little "fantastic journey" into your own body for a moment, exploring the life within, the *force* of life. Imagine yourself shrinking, growing tinier and tinier, until you could fit inside a single one of your cells. What is this cell like? Ponder for a moment the miracle of its creation and the fact that every one of the billions of cells that constitute the physical entity that is you is an incredible feat of engineering, doing its job of keeping you alive and running with maximum efficiency.

7. Realize that this moment of aliveness is simultaneously a moment of ultimate insecurity. Rejoice at the threshold: a new destiny is unfolding. Will you be unable to experience it because you are still bound to the chains of memory and attachment? Or will you shake off these fetters and walk freely into the future, the unknown, the void of possibility? The choice is yours.

8. Now think about the fact that this exercise was an imaginary experience. How do you feel? Grateful, as though you've awakened from a bad dream? Stronger, in realizing that it is possible to emerge from an experience of loss whole and renewed? Think about how many of your fears *are* imaginary. Think about the possibility that nothing is real—cars, houses, jobs, computers—in the sense of being necessary for your ultimate happiness or survival.

You can do this exercise with any dream to which you are greatly attached. Take it further whenever you like. Yes, you can even do it with the person or people you love most in the world. The same steps apply: glory in the dream, feel the anguish of its loss, the beauty of your aliveness, the hope of the new, the unexpected. Along the way, keep the words of the Muslim sage Hadrat Ali in mind:

> Everything quantifiable
> runs out,
> And everything anticipated
> is yet to come.

6

Making the Imagination Shift

Imagination sets us off from the angels. It shows how we have
something they don't have. Maybe they come to hear Mozart be-
cause they don't have any Mozarts. Maybe they come to Chartres
Cathedral because no angel has constructed a cathedral. That's
the human task. This is a kind of gift we make to the angels, the
gift of our art, the gift of our imagination.

MATTHEW FOX, *THE PHYSICS OF ANGELS*

In the physical world, survival is dependent upon eating, drinking,
and breathing; we can't live without our lungs, our digestive systems, all the internal organs that convert food and drink into the
energy necessary to sustain life. In the metaphysical world, however, the most important survival system is the imagination. The
metaphysical world is more present in your life than you may believe. The imagination is the central nervous system of the soul.
We develop strong spiritual bones and muscles when we nourish
the soul with a rich inner life, connecting us to the deeper realms of
the unconscious. Ultimately our imagination allows us an avenue
through which we can ascend to the higher realms of mystical experience.

When we are able to honor our own imagination and understand
just how vitally important it is to us every moment, even in mundane situations, then we will know the imagination as the place

where we meet our mystic selves. It is the place where we can transform our thoughts and ideas into new realities, the place where we can delve into the mysteries of the universe as we explore the ever-changing universe within ourselves.

While the imagination has often been thought of as a child's dimension of make-believe having no place in a reasonable, rational adult world, the truth of the matter is that the imagination is not only a real and valid domain, it is the source of the endless creativity fueling life on Earth; it prompts the changes that assure life's continued technological and spiritual evolution. The great artists and scientists have the utmost reverence for the imagination, for without it they would not have been able to create the literature, paintings, music, art, or theories that continue to improve the world. As quantum physicist Max Planck wrote, "When the pioneer in science sends forth the groping fingers of his thoughts, he must have a vivid, intuitive imagination, for new ideas are not generated by deduction but by an artistically creative imagination."

Albert Einstein is often quoted as stating, "Imagination is more important than knowledge." Why? Because when we think we know something, we usually put an end to the process of learning. We become fixed in our views; we close the door to new possibilities. We need to hear that the imagination is important, for the truth of this statement resonates deep within us. Einstein was ridiculed as an incurable daydreamer as a child and did not do well in school. Most of us had at least one unpleasant experience in school where our imaginations may have been squelched by an imagination-disabled teacher or two.

Great thinkers are intimate with the realm of the imagination, where all things are possible; interestingly enough, this is also, in many spiritual traditions, the realm of God. "All things are possible in him who believes," affirms the New Testament, indicating that an experience of the limitless nature of God also opens the believer to the limitless nature of consciousness. In Hindu tradition the imagination is said to be the birthplace of creativity, from which "the meaning [of existence] bursts forth," and in Buddhism the imagination is considered the doorway to the perception of "all truth." So the imagination, when honored as the realm of the unconscious, is also the realm of both creativity and mystical experience. The more fully one enters into the creative process, the more reverence one accumulates for the mystery of creation, which cannot be explained or known, only discovered again and again, in new forms and ways.

The imagination, then, is a catalyst for change, which in the physical world translates into growth. Change and growth are scary to a lot of people, especially those invested in knowing, that is, in controlling their world so that it doesn't exceed their tight, narrow grasp. People who place a premium on knowing and explaining may treat those who are more imaginative and creatively inclined with distrust. Who can forget poor old Galileo? Yet without him, where would we be today? The same place we would be without our own imagination—rooted in habit, sticks in the mud of fear, deprived of the chance to take our lives into the higher echelons of unlimited possibility. When we reject our imagination and the images with which it tries to speak to us, we stagnate physically, emotionally, spiritually. Yet when we honor our imagination, not only do we grow and change, we stimulate growth and new awareness all around us.

Making an Imagination Shift

Thomas Moore, author of *Care of the Soul,* says, "It's my conviction that slight shifts in imagination have more impact on living than major efforts at change." This is not unlike the Tibetan lama who felt that real miracles have nothing to do with great feats of magic; the true miracle, he maintained, was the liberation of even one single negative emotion. In other words, it's important to respect the pace of learning, the necessity of taking things step-by-step when making changes in both our physical and mental/spiritual realities.

We wouldn't shift directly from first to fourth gear in our car; we have to go through second and third to get to fourth. An imagination shift happens in the same way. Think of the intellect as first gear, the heart as second gear, the spirit as third gear, the soul as fourth gear. We typically live in our intellect, using the information it gives us to make our daily decisions. As we move into the region of the heart, we begin operating from a feeling level, where we experience the first inklings of true compassion, true meaning. From the heart we can proceed to the spirit, the place of inner fire, inspiration, of creative linking to our higher selves. And when we shift into the realm of the imagination, we are in the realm of the soul, a state of oneness not only with the various dimensions of our fragmented selves, but with all of the universe.

What are "slight shifts" in imagination? And why are they so powerful? Basically, we alter our thinking, our perception, through education, through admitting new information into our psyches. Education is typically a gradual, "graded" process; we get information in stages so that we have time to digest it, assimilate it, and use it as a new tool in our lives. Educating our imaginations is no different from educating our intellects. We move into new realms of knowledge bit by bit; if we try to take in too much at once we may experience circuit overload, feeling overwhelmed and unable to understand anything. The imagination is a big country, and as travelers we can't see, experience, and know it in a day trip. The imagination is actually the trip of a lifetime, offering us deeper and deeper, higher and higher levels of perception as we're ready to venture into them.

Slight shifts in imagination involve new ways of seeing. Typically we see things through the filter of our former experience. The way we perceive the world is dependent upon past impression, influence, and habit. And as we perceive the world through past experience, we form expectations of the future based on past experience. Some of these expectations may be reasonable and scientifically sound; others, however, may be limited because they are the result of faulty thinking or false impressions. Making imagination shifts, allowing for new perceptions and possibilities, is a way out of the trap of prejudice and negative thinking that so often prevents humans from achieving a higher consciousness of universal love and compassion. Our ears hear the preaching, but our hearts have trouble internalizing it. Why? Because taken in through the limited physical sense of hearing, the information is doomed to remain an intellectual, not a spiritual, reality. It has not been processed efficiently, as an imagination shift.

Twenty-One Days and Ways to an Imagination Shift

Optimystics delight in making imagination shifts. These shifts can occur anytime, anywhere. Imagination shifting is not difficult; in fact, it often involves the simplest of actions that can offer the most profound rewards. The following can be used as a Twenty-One-Day Plan for making an imagination shift or two in your life. You can use these suggestions for direct action or as food for thought and contemplation. Write about each day in your journal if you are keeping one. Happy shifting!

Day 1: Mind-Wandering Day. This is a day to just let your mind roam free, without censure. Get used to the feel of wandering around in your mind; imagine you're visiting a new country for the first time. You don't want a guided tour; you just want to be able to explore the terrain at your leisure. Bill Gates, the creator of Microsoft, would sit for hours as a child doing nothing except "staring into space." His mother started to worry about him, so she asked him what he was doing during one of these periods of quiet and he said adamantly, "I'm thinking." An insensitive person could have dismissed his hours of thinking as frivolous daydreaming and tried to get him to do something else. We could all use some time to daydream and think. In certain aboriginal cultures there are designated dreamers, members whose main job is to dream the possibilities that other members then can act upon.

As your mind wanders freely, what do you find yourself doing in your mind? Planning for the future? Daydreaming? Worrying?

Fantasizing? Cultivate an awareness of how you habitually use your mind.

Day 2: Image Day. Today, think about the sort of images that dominate your life. What image do you have of yourself, of others, of the world? What images of the present, past, or future bring you pleasure? Discomfort? Think of some images that have helped you in your life and some that have hindered you. Do you understand the power images have to shape your life and your power to re-shape them?

Because we usually give priority to our physical being, we make rules consistent with tangible existence. We demand reality, not fantasy; we want the concrete, not the illusory. We believe what we can see. And yet, what can we and do we see? Nothing more or less than the pictures in our own image-nation, a country into which no one else can really be admitted. When we realize that the images that control us are unique to us, that everyone's reality is different, we begin to have more of a respect for the reality of the imagination and the precious uniqueness of human consciousness.

Day 3: Dream-Catching Day. Dreams are an important way that the imagination works in our lives. Today, begin to take note of your dreams, both waking and sleeping. Can you remember any dreams you had last night or this morning? If so, what were they about? Try exploring them; dialogue with different people or images in them. Was there anything that caused you to experience fear? Joy? Now think about some waking dreams that you have for the future. Write them down.

Day 4: Vision Day. Do you have a vision of your future, your work, your purpose? Are you working toward that vision? Today, use your imagination to think of ways to realize that vision. If any images come to you, write them down. If you don't yet have a vision of your destiny, try setting some time aside today for a mini–vision quest. Take a half hour or more to be by yourself in a quiet place. Do the centering warm-up we talked about in chapter 4. As you breathe and center yourself, feel yourself walking into your imagination, where you will meet an image or a person who will give you some insight into your destiny. Let the experience take you where it will, and use this space to record any insights or revelations.

Day 5: Energy Appreciation Day. We learn to make the most of the boundless source of energy that is always around us, the life force that keeps our hearts beating and the world in motion.

The difference between a person who fully uses his or her imagination and one who doesn't is really only a difference in use of energy. Compared to, say, trees, humans have many ways to use the energy contained in our bodies. We are mobile in various capacities, both physical and mental. And we have keen senses that absorb information around us with miraculous capability. In many ways, human beings are like radios; our senses receive information from the universe and convert it into a form that we can use. Even though we can't see them, the radio waves are all around us all the time; the invisible information is always there, waiting for us to tune in to it. Greatness comes when we learn to tap in to this information through our imaginations, using not just the five physical senses but also our sixth sense, our intuition or psychic radar, to reach new dimensions of awareness, while respecting our bodies so that we can make the best use of the wonders we discover. This is when the miraculous—the conversion of the impossible into the possible, and the possible into reality—occurs. It's like shifting a car from first to fourth gear. We have much more power, much more energy, and we can get to new places faster when we move out of "physical" gear into "imagination" gear.

Day 6: Spirit Day. This is a day to connect to your spirit, the fire within, the voice that leads you in new creative directions. Your spirit is fuel for your passion, which is excitement taken to the next level. What do you feel really passionate about? What lights your fire, sends a rush of energy through you, makes you want to jump up and start the day? Because spirit is akin to fire, you must be careful with it. If you are going to play with fire, it helps to know the basics of fire. Fire needs air and room to burn; water puts it out. Air is connected to thinking and water to feelings and emotionality. Play with the symbolism, then ask yourself, What could be inhibiting your spirit in your life? Optimystics are free spirits—people who free their spirits to explore higher realms of passion, without burning out.

Day 7: Curiosity Day. Imagination and curiosity are in many ways two sides of the same coin. Curiosity leads us to explore new ways of thinking, doing, being. What sorts of things excite your curiosity? What sorts of hopes or dreams get you fired up? What is this saying about you and your personality, your needs? Find something to get excited about. Notice how the feeling of excitement changes your inner and outer chemistry. Spend some time today being curious, which doesn't mean sticking your nose where it doesn't belong. Your nose belongs on you, pointed ahead of you. See where it leads you today.

Day 8: Wonder Day. Wonder is a state of constantly marveling at the great things about life, at the mysteries that are constantly surprising us. Be in wonder today; notice the things that put you in a state of wonder, the things that are really amazing, that make you see above and beyond your own narrow little world of imagined control.

As we move into the optimystic dimension, our sense of wonder becomes highly developed. We begin to feel reverence for life, for the unknown, the unexplored, the possible. We don't assume that we have all the answers; instead, we celebrate the questions. And in so doing, something interesting begins to happen. The humdrum, the predictable, the expected begins to give way to the miraculous. Contemplate how the imagination is the most direct avenue to the miraculous. By definition, a miracle is an extraordinary event considered to be a manifestation of divine or supernatural power, an event that excites awe and wonder. The word *miracle* comes from the Latin *mirari*, "to wonder at," which, as you might have deduced, is also the origin of the word *mirror*. In a mirror we wonder at ourselves, at that other that is us, at the miracle of union between these two separate selves, each gazing upon the other, each the same. We *wonder*. And where do we typically do our wondering? In our imaginations.

Day 9: Doubt Day. This is a day to explore your doubts. Doubt isn't all bad; sometimes it's a necessary cautionary tool. But too much doubt inhibits the imagination and the possibilities for change in our lives. Are you the kind of doubter who, like Thomas, just needed the evidence in order to believe? Or are you the kind of doubter who's always setting up roadblocks in the path of possibility, who's always raining on someone else's imagination party? Where do your doubts lie? Where do they come from? Do you doubt that certain dreams can come true, and if so, why?

Day 10: Play Day. Play is vital to children because it helps them develop the life skills they'll need to navigate in an adult world. Remember that play is a source of joy and energy that is equally important to adults. Today, reconnect to your imagination through play. Accept the validity of play as an exercise in freeing the spirit and the imagination. Figure out a way to have your own playtime, or spend some time with a child in play. If you like, have some Gestalt therapy fun and play with a hunk of clay, letting your imagination become the sculptor, bringing your unconscious to light. Realize that the clay is symbolic of your own life, which is not constant, stagnant, or inert but rather malleable, shifting, open to reformation.

Day 11: No-Limit Day. What limits have you put on your imagination, on your dream power? What boundaries have you drawn around your image-nation? Think about why. Then, just for today, erase those limits. Begin to shift from finite to infinite gear. Realize that like the clay, the territory of the imagination is ever changing, ever changeable, and that it can be expanded or contracted simply according to your attitude. Get into the feeling of being or doing anything. What images, desires, or emotions come up?

Day 12: Why-Not Day. Expand your horizons today. Why not do something you've been meaning to do or have been afraid to do? Today, put yesterday's exercise to work. Take a why-not action in any area of your life and see what happens. Don't be afraid to wonder why and to tap into the limitless world of possibilities.

Day 13: Enchantment Day. To enchant means to "surround with song," as well as to bring delight or cast a spell over something. What do you find enchanting—creating a song within you, casting a spell of joy around you? Have you been a prisoner of the ordinary for too long? Could your soul use a sprinkling of fairy dust? Today, open your imagination to the invisible realms and bring some enchantment into your life in whatever way strikes your fancy.

Day 14: Intuition Day. Today is a day to tune in to your intuition. Pick an area of your life or a potential action about which you are confused or uncertain. Settle down and listen to your intuition. Think about times in the past when you listened to your intuition and were glad you did or when you ignored your intuition and were sorry. There is a difference between intuition and unfounded fear or wishful thinking; see if you can separate these matters. Both fear and intuition can be motivating forces. Our intuition is rarely based on fear; it is a still, small voice that tugs at you in your gut. A fear can be traced back to a worry; it is something that hasn't happened and can be used as a simple caution sign. Exercising intuition without excess baggage takes lots of practice and the willingness to not look back in regret.

Day 15: Unconditional Trust Day. In what areas of your life might you need to have more trust? What's keeping you from trusting? Have you thought about trust lately? Think about why you trust the people you trust. Is it because they do what you want them to, or is it because you love them and can accept that they won't always play by your rules? Are you having trouble trusting God for conditional reasons? Are you testing God to see if God will meet your conditions so you can safely trust? Is God not playing by your rules? Is your sense of trust strictly conditional? Today is your day to let go of any conditions you have put on the universe and to learn to trust yourself. Don't forget that trusting yourself means trusting that you have the strength to face the unknown by trusting God. The best way to trust God is to surrender your pride and strict conditions and admit to yourself that trust is an ongoing lesson in life.

Day 16: Soul Retrieval Day. Has your soul wandered off in any way because you forgot to give it its chicken soup? If so, take today to hunt it down and bring it home. Think about who or what your soul is with, where it feels most content, to whom or what it feels most connected. How can you feed it the daily food it wants so it won't wander off again? Ask your soul outright what it wants. If you don't get an answer right away, just stay tuned; the answer may not be a verbal one. The soul speaks to us in many ways, and we need to be creative with our hearing. Ask, and if you spend the day consciously aware of your soul, you will receive an answer.

Day 17: Letting Go Day. Today, temporarily let go of any growth-inhibiting emotions such as regret, guilt, bitterness, envy, and any other emotions that leave you feeling stuck. First notice these feelings inside yourself. Take a few minutes to explore them. What do you think they're doing for you? What do you think they aren't doing for you? Why are you hanging on to them? What would happen if you let them go? In your imagination, release them, feel yourself growing lighter and lighter, and see where you go from here.

Day 18: Active Imagination Day. Carl Jung did a great deal of work with the process of active imagination, which refers to meeting and talking with the different parts of ourselves that we may or may not be aware of but that influence us unconsciously throughout our lives. Today, spend some time in active imagination. Pick a situation in your life that is bothering you or about which you would like some clarity. Close your eyes and go into your imagination. What figures or images come to you? Begin talking to them. If you don't see anyone clearly but you hear a voice, dialogue with that voice. Write down what transpires between you.

Day 19: Beauty Day. Today is a day of exploring what the concept of beauty means to you and how to create more of it. Where is the spirit of beauty in your life? Which areas need an infusion of beauty? How might negative thoughts be preventing you from noticing the beauty that already exists? Pick a "beauty project" today; start noticing and creating beauty for yourself in ways that will uplift the environment and your spirit.

Day 20: Magic Day. Become a magician today. How do you view magic? Is it illusion? Miracle? Supernatural? The optimystic understands the difference between imaginative magic, which is the transformation that we can work in our lives through the power of our own creative resources, and magical thinking, which is a nonproductive form of fantasy in which we rely on mere beliefs to change a situation instead of relying on our own ability to shift our perspective. Imaginative magic means that we take a proactive approach and change our attitude, or consciously let go of a fruitless fantasy. Be the author of your own magic. Let symbols and things you notice around you—like a beautiful cloud formation—become good omens of hope and magic. Where would you like to work a little magic in your life? Take a situation that's bothersome or unsatisfactory and see how you might change it by changing your attitude toward it or by simply giving it over to your imagination.

Day 21: Mystic Celebration Day. The mystics celebrate life as being perfect in God's eyes. Today, realize that your life is perfect in its unfolding. Look back on what you've accomplished in these last twenty-one days; think about the change that's always occurring, the surprises that are always ahead thanks to your imagination. Let today be a day of mystic celebration, sheer delight in the wonder of your existence and the gift of your imagination. Create your own day of ritual, reflection, and partying. Get into the mystic spirit of life!

7

Time Is on Our Side

In this attention, time . . . has become quiet and still. In this stillness there is an immeasurable, not comparable movement, a movement that has no being; that's the essence of bliss and death and life. . . .

KRISHNAMURTI ON MEDITATION, *ORDINARY MAGIC*

Optimystics are not slaves of time. They know that time is not a possession, that a spiritual moment can transpire in two seconds and seem like hours. If the optimist says, "I have all the time in the world," the optimystic says, "I have all the time in and *out of* the world." Optimystics delight in the knowledge that time is not linear, that the timeless moment of the mystic consciousness is as real as any clock-oriented measure of time. Optimystics realize that time is on our side—that time as we perceive it is a limitation belonging to the earth plane. On the other side, in the metaphysical dimension, time is completely fluid.

Has time ever seemed to stand still in your life? To drag? To fly? Have you ever had the experience of moving outside or beyond time? Has ordinary time ever seemed to expand or contract in strange, inexplicable ways? It is possible that time has no meaning other than that which we attach to it.

On one level, time itself is an entirely empirical, unalterable fact. The measurable speed of seconds, minutes, hours, days, and years always remains the same, scientifically and mathematically speaking. So when you find yourself experiencing time at different speeds and levels, it is an entirely subjective experience. Time may seem to fly on some days or to drag on other days, but from a mathematical perspective it never changes. So it is not the fact of time but *how we experience time* that determines its power in our lives.

The dictionary defines *time* in several different ways. In its first meaning, time is "all the years of the past, present, and future—the passing of these taken as a whole." And the literal definition is: "a nonspatial continuum in which events occur in apparently irreversible succession." That word *irreversible* jumps out. If we believe in it, we become fearful that time is rushing ahead and passing us by. In the great war of life versus death, time marches on relentlessly, trampling all who stand in its path. But then there is that word *apparently,* indicating that perhaps this definition of time is not the conclusive one; perhaps there is another way of looking at it. And the fact is that to date, scientists have not been able to show that time flows in a linear, irreversible direction. Nobel Prize–winning physicist Richard Feynman admitted that the nature of time is difficult and that we may be questioning time for a very long time. And Einstein's theory of relativity blew apart all traditional notions of time, opening up the possibility of everything from states of no time to simultaneous realities.

The Rhythm Method of Time

In music, keeping time means keeping a beat. The beat is the skeleton on which the music is hung. It is the necessary internal structure. When we keep time, we keep the beat of life alive. So time doesn't keep us when we keep it. We have a natural rhythm, just as nature does. We have different rhythms in our daily lives, such as sleep and wakefulness. All of our rhythms are affected by one another; that is, our heartbeat may be affected by the rhythm of our work or the traffic around us or the music we are listening to.

Optimystics find ways to time themselves to their own biological rhythms. Nature is often our best teacher. If we feel life is speeding by too quickly, we can watch how cats spend their days, how the birds pass time, how the sun moves so gracefully across the sky, how gently night falls, and we can remind ourselves that we too are a part of nature.

Great things come to us through following the natural rhythm of the cycles of nature. Dark nights of the soul seem to magically change as the sun comes up. When we are grieving or in a state of pain, we are told that the greatest healer is time, that "in time" we will be whole again. One of the most beautiful things about time is that it allows us to change for the better, that throughout our lives we can evolve and, like alchemists, turn our lead into gold. In this way time becomes reversible.

Sometimes we need to step outside of our ruts and routines to remind us that time is not our master. We can so easily become slaves of habit—of habitual time—that we need to shake up our routines once in a while to remember that we can always deal with time differently. For instance, if you always get up a 6 A.M. sharp, try getting up a little earlier as a symbolic gesture. If you are used to eating at a certain time, eat at another time just to prove to yourself that you *can* change time. With conscious attention, do everything in your day a little earlier than planned; then observe how changing your routine affects everything around you. Pay attention to how odd time can seem as you venture through the day. Have you ever found yourself in a time warp, a place where time stands still and, quite suddenly, nothing seems to make sense? These experiences should alert you to the fact that any and all notions of time are up for grabs.

People in Los Angeles joke that they measure distance not in miles but in the time it takes to get somewhere by driving the freeway. People who fly a lot certainly know how far New York is from their residence in hours and minutes; for them distance is measured in flying time. Back in the days of horses, people would have thought of time in terms of how fast a horse could get them to their destination. Although we don't think about it, when we make a phone call across the country, time is traveling almost at the speed of light.

There is a sacred sense of aliveness that we can experience at any moment, as soon as we wean ourselves from the insidious habit of clock watching. If you find yourself noticing the time too often during the day, start trusting your psyche. It knows what time it is. Haven't you had the experience of waking up right before your alarm clock was about to go off? As we begin to trust our inner clocks and allow ourselves to be more flexible about time, schedules, and appointments, we usually find that a strange and wonderful thing happens: suddenly we have more time! We begin to understand that time doesn't control us, but that we can control it, make it move faster or slower, expand or contract it. What a freeing idea!

So the next time you're tempted to go by dictionary definitions, realize that you can look at and experience the universe in many different ways. And when Webster says time is "apparently irreversible," you can say, "Apparently not!" Time is not fixed but malleable; through our inner changes we *can* change time. We can go "back to the future" or forward to the present. We can find our own rhythm method of time and march to the optimystic beat of that proverbial different drummer.

Does Time Ever Run Out?

When we believe that time is like a conveyor belt carrying us mindlessly and irreversibly toward extinction, then we live with a companion named fear. We also live with the notion that we will run out of time. We often hear people talk about the quality of life being more important than its quantity. This can be a comforting platitude for those who don't have a large quantity of time left. Let's face it: quantity of life *is* important, especially if we feel we have a lot to accomplish and to offer. But quantity without quality is not the goal.

Defining life by the amount of time one has is meaningless. Typically we think that someone who has lived a long life is fortunate. The death of a child or a young person is usually regarded as cause for great remorse and bitterness: "She never had a chance—cut down in the prime of life." "He hadn't even begun to live." We talk of death in terms of one's "time": "It wasn't his time"; "it was her time." Yet, as we know, those with relatively short life spans have often been the ones who made the most impact on history and touched most deeply the lives of those around them. Think about Mozart, Anne Frank, or any young person you have met who left early, yet left an indelible effect on you.

It is natural for us to want to have as much time as possible on Earth. But we can take great comfort in the fact that our souls and spirits *do* transcend time. Anne Frank, as she sat hidden in her attic room—effectively dead to the world in the effort to become invisible to the Nazis—wrote in her diary: "I want to go on living even after my death! And therefore I am grateful to God for giving me this gift, this possibility of developing myself, and of writing, of expressing all that is within me." It's as if somehow she knew that what she was writing in her youthful diary would reverberate for years to come, outliving her body but not her spirit. Mozart wrote music that could only be heard live in the moment. Did he ever dream that someday, hundreds of years later, people would still be enjoying his music all over the world, at any hour, simply by pressing a button or turning a dial? Anne Frank and Mozart live on; in a curious way they are even more alive than they were during their lifetimes, proving that time, in the sense of an irreversible succession of hours, days, weeks, months, years culminating in death, really has no meaning. If we use time now to its fullest, as the raw material with which to create our spiritual legacy, we will accomplish the feat of transcending time. We can truly become eternal, in the sense of spiritual time, continuing to affect life on Earth after we have left it.

Since time is one of those things we can't stop, all we can do is to become a part of it so that we too are timeless. This doesn't mean that we have to be famous, die young, or create a lasting piece of art. In each of our lives we are creating moments of love that touch the hearts of others. The good news is that a simple moment of love can have a timeless effect on the world, and we have the capacity to create and choose love in each action we take.

To become timeless we have to *feel* timeless. Our bodies show us that we are part of time, because time changes our bodies. Aging can be accepted as a natural and beautiful process or as a futile and aggressive fight against time. Seeing life as a continual process of evolution, not dissolution, helps us to break free of time's tight grip.

Optimystics work at extricating themselves from standard beliefs about aging. The body is a temporary dwelling; we all agree that it will die. Yet many act as if the body is their only reality, and they try desperately to preserve it forever. When asked his age, Paramahansa Yogananda would reply, "I never tell people my age, because I can't. I am ageless. When people ask me, How old are you?, they are asking, How old is your body? But I am not my body. The body is only a house. When you ask someone how old they are, do you say, how old is your house?" So, think of a new way to approach the process of aging. One way is to think of ourselves as ripening. We start out as hard fruit and then in time ripen to a soft sweetness.

At Present

An optimystic is not just living in the moment, but living in the mystic moment, the spiritual moment. Spiritual moments are like babies: there's one born every six seconds. They occur when we least expect them, and they occur anytime we are willing to create them. Anything can become a spiritual moment. We may experience a moment when we suddenly experience the presence of a loving divine force of which we are an inextricable part and we realize that love is a constant, that the inherent beauty in life is eternal even when it is temporarily obscured from view. A spiritual moment may be a bona fide epiphany, an instantaneous, life-altering enlightenment such as Saul experienced on the way to Damascus. Or it may be as simple as seeing, for the first time, the divine artistry of a leaf falling from a tree or the spark of soul that radiates from a loved one's eyes.

Most of us go through life ensconced in the comfortable, protective gear of habit. We do things on autopilot, without thinking, without noticing. The quintessential mystic command, "Be here now," falls on deaf ears as we scramble to deal with the ups and downs of life. At times, we are so far from the here and now that we might as well be on the moon. Even while we're stationary, our minds are time-traveling like crazy, bouncing from past to future like a Ping-Pong ball as we relive events long gone and fantasize about events to come. Meanwhile, the present slips past us.

Sometimes it seems as if we are doing time here on Earth, stuck in a prison for a reason we don't know. In this state we are waiting for time to pass, waiting for the future that may or may not come. As poor Richard II lamented, as he languished in prison, "I wasted time, and now time doth waste me." If we want to free ourselves from the imprisonment of time, our only choice is not to "kill time" but to change our underlying attitude toward and perception of this moment in time. The most holy attribute of time is that it is change, and change brings awareness of new avenues we can travel in each moment.

Moments of pure awareness make us one with the now. When our minds are focused, when we are truly paying attention, we are rewarded with the supreme gift of the present. But when we allow our minds to wander off into the thickets and brambles of worry and fear or down the yellow brick road of the rosy future, the present moment—which, ironically, is the only thing we have—is lost forever.

Timing, Synchronicity, and Destiny

If we believe in fate and destiny, then we believe that our soul has certain things it is programmed to experience. This could be due to reincarnation, astrology, or the unique experience of our own DNA encoded with messages from our ancestors. We could say that our soul holds the keys to our destiny and fate, to the mysterious path we are drawn along in life, finding ourselves in so many amazing situations. Let's say that our spirit represents our free will, our capacity to not be locked into any one particular destiny or way of being. We can lift ourselves off of the wheel of karma, so to speak, and choose to rise above our fate. This happens naturally when we enlighten our consciousness.

How do we know when we should choose to override the fate of the soul? What happens if we are so filled with spirit that we find ourselves trying to force events and push destiny? Although these are mysterious questions that will never be answered in absolutes, they are fun to play around with. To balance soul and spirit we need to honor both. Too much striving to go beyond our soul or our attachment to life, in other words, too much use of our free will to bypass lessons, tends to create problems. Too much spirit can cause too much struggle; too much complacency can make us a victim of time. In other words, although we create our own destiny by our choices and attitude, there are things we are here to experience. The lessons of the soul are not always fun and joyful, and sometimes we wonder why should we have to suffer such trials. But in the long run we can take from every experience a great truth. And *then* we can use the power of our spirit to lead us in a positive direction.

One by-product of being awake and spiritual is that we encounter meaningful coincidences or synchronistic events. These are events that seem to hold a magical meaning; they go beyond what would be expected by random chance. You've probably had the experience of thinking about someone you hadn't seen for a long time and encountering them "just by chance" a day or two later. Or perhaps you dropped a book and it fell open to a page that held precisely the information you were looking for. When these synchronicities, as Jung called them, happen, we can feel our destinies in process. We have a form of proof that our lives are guided by forces that are not always "sensible"—of the senses—or explainable. Knowing that the mystery is alive and that something else is always going on under the guise of everyday life is an exciting antidote to the boring notion of the relentless, predictable march of time.

Yet we have to be discerning when we experience synchronicities, realizing that sometimes these amazing coincidences are only representations of opportunities and possibilities or reminders that we are on track. While optimystics are always open to synchronicity and the miracle of the unexpected, they also use their intuition and natural guidance in deciding what exactly to do with the magic the universe provides. In other words, if we focus only on the magical aspects of synchronicities, we may miss the message and the messenger.

Time is on our side—*only* on our side. If we allow ourselves to be more in tune with our mystic selves, we will be able to live out our spiritual moment in an eternity that we agreed to before our birth. We fear death because we think that it has something to do with time. But every mystic, and every optimystic, knows that we won't be stuck in time when we cross over to the other side. This means that our loved ones who have gone before us are really with us, and we are with them. In fact, everything may be happening all at the same time, simultaneously, eternally, never ending. It's enough to make us want to smash a clock!

8

Basic Training in Tragedy Management

Tragedy wonderfully reveals the nature of man.

JOHN KENNETH GALBRAITH

If you want to get a good idea of the absurdity of life on Earth, just think about the concept of tragedy. To some people, a tragedy is the loss of a loved one, a home, or a homeland; to others it's a hotel without room service or the Dallas Cowboys winning another Super Bowl. Some humans survive holocausts, pestilence, atomic bombs, and other horrific devastations and still manage to find meaning in life; others think their latest hangnail is front-page news. In many ways, the concept of tragedy is proof that God has a sense of humor and that the mystic belief in the perfection of all things, good or bad, sane or insane, is the only way to fly. How else could one navigate safely in this giant Mad Hatter's tea party, where all too often nobody seems to be able to connect to anyone else's pain because all are off in their own delusory little world?

In order to come to terms with tragedy, we first have to know what it is and what it isn't. The classic definition of a tragedy is "a dramatic, disastrous event of moral significance." *Othello* depicts a tragedy. The Holocaust was a tragedy. The sinking of the Titanic was a tragedy. All three came about because of some gross moral flaw in someone's personality; Othello was blinded by jealousy, Hitler was blinded by hatred and self-importance, the men responsible for the Titanic's demise were blinded by greed, a desire for glory, and a false belief in their invincibility. Each of these moral flaws resulted in needless death.

In this way, tragedy acquires a bit of a perspective, perhaps one that we've never considered. Say a child dies of cancer. To all outward appearances, this would seem a great tragedy. But since there was no moral cause of death, since the death was, in essence, beyond anyone's power to control or circumvent, is it a tragedy? Or is it just a terribly painful experience?

The child's death would be a tragedy if those who were affected by it could not meet and move past their grief. If the parents were driven to despair or even suicide, this would be a tragedy. If, on the other hand, some good came out of the death—if the parents began a fund to support a children's hospital or dedicated their lives to helping others recover from similar loss—then *tragedy* would not necessarily be an apt word to describe the event. A chief distinguishing characteristic of tragedy is its finality, its unchangeability. Death is the ultimate finality. But is death really a tragedy? Isn't it our response to death that determines whether or not it falls into the realm of the tragic or the realm of, to use *The Book of Runes* author Ralph Blum's potent phrase, "opportunity disguised as loss"? In this way, perhaps there is no event that, in and of itself, is a tragedy. Who knows?

To the optimystic, tragedy is compounded when we are unable to learn from it. And, to some extent, tragedies may be only as devastating as our perception of them. That is why even the most horrendous atrocities have failed, time and again, to extinguish the eternal flame of the human spirit. It is only when we allow that flame to go out in our lives—when we ourselves extinguish it, because we are the only ones who *can* extinguish it—that the angels weep for the pain that we were unable to transcend, the light that we were unable to see. So the first step in managing tragedy might be to do a little imagination shifting, to glimpse tragedy in a way that takes it out of the narrow context of pain and suffering and into its larger context, as life's most powerful agent of transformation.

This Is a Test . . . This Is Only a Test . . .

The people who are able to rise above tragedy or pain are those who somehow can view their difficult experience as a test of courage, will, and commitment to life. We've all heard of somebody who's been through the worst thing we could ever imagine and has come out the other side. We wonder, How could they do that? What makes them want to survive? The human spirit is a wonderfully mysterious thing. It seems to be living proof of the possibility of resurrection—the fact that even if part of us dies as the result of a devastating loss, we still have the power within us to emerge from the experience in some way reborn.

One of the best ways to manage tragedy is to learn how others have managed it successfully. When we're looking for a way to cope with our own sorrow, nothing beats inspirational stories of personal triumph in the face of loss. Here's one of our favorites:

Theodore Roosevelt came into the world a sickly infant who, by all rights, never should have lived. He struggled with a childhood asthma so debilitating that many nights he didn't even have the extra breath needed to blow out his bedside candle. His entire childhood was essentially consumed in a constant battle to breathe. But his father, a strong and loving man with an incredible will, encouraged Theodore to take life by the horns, not to give in to self-pity or fear. The elder Roosevelt walked the floors with the boy in his arms during the long nights when he couldn't sleep because of lack of air. He made his son work out with weights to build up his scrawny asthmatic chest, and he took him on long summer hikes through the Adirondacks. He encouraged him to explore his interests and to be passionate about them. And somehow, the boy beat the odds and made it to adulthood, Harvard, marriage, fatherhood, and a promising career as a politician.

Then, on February 14, 1884, at the age of twenty-six, Theodore Roosevelt suffered a loss of incredible immensity. In one night, his beloved young wife died of kidney failure following the birth of their first child, and his beloved mother died of typhoid upstairs in the same house. Accounts tell of the distraught young man running up and down the stairs, trying to be with both of the dying women at once. Roosevelt was completely devastated. "The light has gone out of my life," he wrote in his diary.

Talk about tragedy! Now Roosevelt was at a crossroads. He could fold up and die. He could become bitter and self-destructive. Instead, he chose to literally "ride out" his agony by going out West for several years and becoming a cowboy! With his spectacles, Harvard accent, and upper-crust Eastern ways, Roosevelt was an immediate object of scorn to the rough-and-tumble residents of the Dakota plains, who nearly fell over laughing at his pearl-handled guns and expensive designer cowboy shirts. But he eventually won the real cowboys' respect with his incredible will and determination. He wanted to prove, to himself and everybody else, that he had what it took to tough it out, to face himself and his grief in the bleakest of environments, and to emerge all the stronger for it.

You know the rest. Roosevelt became, among other things, one of the country's most energetic and admired presidents, a man of enormous charm, courage, and personal integrity. He remarried, had four more children, and kept them and the country on the go with his humor, wit, and irrepressible love of life. "It's hard," wrote historian David McCullough, "to imagine anyone living life with more passionate intensity."

You'll undoubtedly agree that this is an extraordinary example of tragedy management. Of course, Roosevelt wasn't perfect; in his rabid pursuit of male vigor, to which he turned to offset the pain of his loss, he became, at times, a tyrant who grew more and more opinionated in his older age. But the fact remains that when faced with the kind of loss that many people would not have been able to cope with, Roosevelt chose to turn the loss into an opportunity for new life. And so, in the optimystic's estimation, tragedy was averted.

Roosevelt is a perfect example of the "tragic optimist," a term coined by Holocaust survivor Viktor Frankl. In 1946, Frankl's small book, *Man's Search for Meaning,* was published in Austria, then translated into English in 1959. Fifty years later it has been published in some nineteen languages, has sold over two million copies, and has become something of a guidepost for living in our shaky post-Holocaust, pre-Apocalypse world.

Frankl was a medical doctor and psychotherapist who survived Auschwitz and other concentration camps. As a result of his terrible experiences, Frankl was able not only to make some sort of sense out of his and the sufferings of millions, but also to create a new form of psychoanalysis. His "logotherapy" is designed to help people focus not on the past but on the present and the future, not on their neuroses but on the meaning that life holds for them and the actions they can take to realize that meaning.

It may seem astonishing that life could hold such meaning for a man who witnessed the worst in humanity, whose sufferings could not be measured by any reasonable yardstick, who lost nearly everything and everyone dear to him—including his treasured twenty-four-year-old wife—during the Nazi reign of terror. Yet as Frankl himself observed,

> Man's search for meaning is the primary motivation in his life and not a "secondary realization" of instinctual drives. . . . Any attempt to restore a man's inner strength in the camp had first to succeed in showing him some future goal. Nietzsche's words, "He who has a *why* to live can bear with almost any *how*" could be the guiding model for all psychotherapeutic efforts regarding prisoners.

Frankl sums up the impetus for logotherapy, and for living, in the term *tragic optimism,* which, in essence, is the ability of a human being to remain hopeful in the face of pain, suffering, and death, to turn negatives into positives, to grow with, not against, the grain of circumstance.

So what matters, says Frankl, "is the ability to make the best of any given situation. The 'best,' however, is that which in Latin is called *optimum;* hence we speak of a tragic optimism. It is an optimism in the face of tragedy, for it keeps in sight the human potential, which at its best always allows for (1) turning suffering into a human achievement and accomplishment; (2) deriving from guilt the opportunity to change oneself for the better; and (3) deriving from life's transitoriness an incentive to take responsible action."

In other words, one needs to go beyond oneself into the larger picture of one's place in the universe, one's own unique role in the drama of human existence, in order to move beyond *suffering* and into *living,* beyond *surviving* and into *thriving.* Only then can we understand the deeper dimensions of the reason for our existence and appreciate it in the larger context of a spiritual destiny. Only then can one become an optimist in the purest sense of the term. And, when we combine this tragic optimism with the experience of moving beyond the confines of the present into the boundless dimensions of the infinite, feeling the peace of union with a greater truth that some call God, we become optimystics.

If you have suffered loss, or what you perceive of as tragedy in your life, how did you respond to it? If you accept it as a test, how did you score? Are there any events in your life that seemed like tragedies at the time but that, in retrospect, turned out to have their own meaning and purpose in your life? How did you grow from the experience? What good things were brought to you in the space that loss left open?

The Right to Grieve

However valid the truth that tragedy is opportunity disguised as loss, it does not ease the pain of that loss. While we may, as optimystics, strive for spiritual liberation in the face of loss, we know that this isn't a shortcut. Before we can accept the hidden blessings, we must first go through the very physical process of grief, allowing ourselves to feel and deal with our loss.

Optimystics don't try to talk themselves or anyone else out of pain. Instead, they advocate facing the pain, sitting with it, going into it, realizing that, since grief is the new companion that will be with us for a while, it is to our advantage to get to know it. An interesting fact about grief is that when we meet it head-on, it becomes in some strange way our friend, teacher, and guide on what may be the most torturous—and illuminating—journey of our lives.

In surrendering to our grief—allowing it to take us by the hand as a friend and to govern our days, and allowing it in the darkness—we are, in a way, letting it work strange magic on us in deep, unknowable ways. Often in times of great loss we are so fragile, so weak and worn out, that we simply don't have the strength to fight sorrow. When we surrender to it and permit it to take us where it will, grief will guide us to the very depths of our soul, a foreign region we might never have visited before. Out of grief arises compassion. Out of loss arises spiritual awareness. Out of death arises a new respect for life. The deeper we allow ourselves to go into our grief, the better we can work with it, process it, and reshape it into new forms of being. We have to learn to trust it, letting it take us slowly and carefully through the long and arduous process of shock, denial, numbness, despair, and, finally, acceptance with uncanny precision. There is a method to the madness of life and death; it is in grief that we discover that method and our own extraordinary resources for survival and renewal.

Know That You Matter

One of the most difficult things about loss is the loss of energy and enthusiasm for life that so often accompanies it. When we face the forbidding rite of passage that tragedy commands us to undergo, how can we survive it if we don't have the necessary physical and emotional resources?

To achieve any level of inner peace we must, as the saying goes, take one day at a time. We really have no other choice. As we do so, we find that some days are better than others. If one day or week we feel absolutely rotten to the core, the next may cause us to feel the faintest stirrings toward life once again. So we gradually reconnect to our sense of hope, the power source that keeps humanity running when everything else fails.

In order to be able to feel hope, however, we must be able to feel, on some level, that we matter. When life seems too difficult to bear, when the thought of death, of escape, becomes too sweet, it is only our sense of purpose, our sense of mattering, that will pull us back from the abyss of self-destruction. As Viktor Frankl says, what tragedy requires from us, ultimately, is that we discover the "why" of our lives—why we are here, why we matter, why we should go on living. If we don't, then *we* are the tragedy, not the event that propelled us over the edge.

The optimystic knows that none of us are accidents. Every one of us has a destiny to fulfill. Therefore, it is vital in times of tragedy to remind ourselves of the tremendous opportunity we have, in this searing moment, to discover the answer to our own personal, existential "Why?" This is a perfect topic for contemplation, a perfect mantra. "Whyyyyyy . . ." Chant it as you meditate, breathe it in and out, let it fill your muscles and bones and blood. An answer will come—an answer that may surprise you and turn your life around forever.

Within tragedy lie the seeds of our destiny. In fact, tragedy and destiny go hand in hand. It may be destiny that we experience loss when we do. We don't know why; it's part of the mystery that optimystics accept as the grand surprise package. Through tragedy we may discover our destiny, our purpose, our why. Once we are able to rise up from our grief and decide that it is, indeed, time to live again, we will be ready to make a new passage into a new unknown. It helps to know that we are important in the great scheme of things and that how we reshape our lives from the raw material of pain is of extreme significance, both to ourselves and to others who may be stumbling along the same rough path. As every optimystic knows, nothing that we do goes unnoticed by God. We have an effect that radiates throughout the universe; we have a responsibility to the life force of which we are a part. As Sogyal Rinpoche entreats us, in *The Tibetan Book of Living and Dying,*

Don't let us half die with our loved ones. . . . Let us try to live after they have gone, with greater fervor. Let us try, at least, to fulfill the dead person's wishes or aspirations in some way. . . . Bereavement can force you to look at your life directly, compelling you to find a purpose in it where there may not have been one before. . . . Pray for help and strength and grace. Pray you will survive and discover the richest possible meaning to the new life you now find yourself in.

9

When Was the Last Time a Hopeless Person Inspired You?

How can you be hopeless?
I am growing in you with my ever-luminous
and ever fulfilling Dream.

SRI CHINMOY

Hope is probably the most necessary attitude for humans to keep alive—and to keep them alive. Hope is paramount to the art of living productively. In his book *Learned Optimism*, psychologist Martin Seligman analyzes the many studies that have shown that hopelessness is the single most dangerous aspect of depression, for it is "the one most accurate predictor of suicide." Seligman also discovered an interesting fact: that children under the age of seven cannot sustain a sense of hopelessness. They may experience depression but not despair. So we can make the hopeful conclusion that hope is natural to humans and sustained hopelessness is not.

The Three Rules of Hope

Rule #1: There is always hope. When we are down, many of us don't dare to believe there is always hope, because we are so afraid of having our hopes dashed. But hope is a natural component of life, as natural as the human organism itself. We have something akin to a hope gene, which is a far more brilliant and valuable commodity than the Hope Diamond. So take comfort in the knowledge that hope is already in you; you were born with it.

Rule #2: Hope is our right. We have a right to be hopeful at all times, no matter how dire our circumstances may seem. To the optimystic, there is really no such thing as false hope; all hope has its purpose, even if it is simply to afford us the luxury of denial necessary for us to go through a period of great difficulty. When we have hope, we continue going, even if we're not quite sure of the direction we're going in. Without hope, however, we cannot muster up the inner reserves necessary to emerge past misfortune or frustration.

Rule #3: Hope fuels joy. Joy is the energy that life runs on. We are not only entitled to joy; we are requested by God to rejoice in life and to spread the good feeling around. Joy is a feeling of vitality that motivates us to pursue the things that make us happy and fulfilled. Without hope, how can we have joy? Without hope, how can we give others a sense of joy or even the glimmer of its wondrous transformative possibilities?

The Seven Most Ineffective Habits of Highly Hopeless People

1. *Humorlessness.* It is a fact that with humor there cannot be hopelessness. The reverse is also true: with humorlessness, there cannot be hope. Some people refuse to see the humor in anything, especially themselves, and try to get you to put a frown on your face along with them. Take this as a warning, and keep your distance.

2. *Indulging in destructive criticism.* Some criticism can be helpful and is necessary in our lives. But when people take it upon themselves to remind you at all times what you are doing wrong and how you can do it better, or when they advise you to give up because you'll never be any good at it anyway, what they're really saying is, "You're hopeless." This is simply projection; they're the ones who are hopeless, that is, unable to feel hope and spread it around.

3. *Lack of vision.* Hopeless people have a tendency to insist that reality consists only of what they themselves can see with their own two eyes. Hopeless people are not good at glimpsing alternatives and possibilities beyond what's in their immediate visual field. The only trouble is, they have a big blind spot: their ingrained sense of hopelessness. This often leads them to fatalistic conclusions.

4. *Believing in the virtues of suffering.* Hopeless people put a lot of stock in suffering, especially theirs. After all, when you're hopeless you're always suffering. And there's so much to suffer over—who has the *time* to be happy or cheerful? Suffering gives the hopeless person two big advantages: attention from others and an excuse not to open their optimystic lesson book. Being hopeless is a form of laziness; it's much easier to suffer and blame God or whoever for your misery than it is to get up off your behind and actively pursue a path to contentment and compassion. So if you're around someone who makes you feel like you've just found a black hole and want to crawl into it, surround yourself—and that person—in plenty of white light and beat it out of that energy field!

5. *Buying into negative statistics.* We are a statistic-obsessed society. This wouldn't be so bad if we used the negative ones as a motivation to go out and improve ourselves and the world. But hopeless people use negative statistics to make themselves and those around them more paranoid and fearful. Hopeless people refuse to realize that there's always the other half of the statistic. If 50 percent of people die of a certain type of cancer within five years, this means that 50 percent don't. A hopeless person will think, "Half of all the people die; I'm doomed." A hopeful person will look at the glass as half full, saying "Fifty percent of people survive; I can too." They may not, but they'll sure make the world a less dismal place while they're around. And they just may survive, because statistics also show that a positive attitude gives people a better chance of beating the odds in serious or life-threatening situations.

6. *Repressing emotions.* While some hopeless people are extremely verbal about their despair or bitterness, to the chagrin of their fellow humans, others suffer in silence. They deny and repress anger and sadness as well as joy and enthusiasm. As a result, their spirits are dampened; picture a Sherman tank rolling over them! Hopeless people have a pervading sense of the futility of it all. So they don't bother expressing their real feelings, because "what good will it do? It will only upset others if I

get mad or cry or tell them the truth. If I get excited about something, somebody will shoot me down." Ironically, what a hopeless person doesn't realize is that once we get in touch with our real feelings—our real needs—and begin to express them, the fog of hopelessness that has hung over our lives and obscured our optimystic vision magically begins to lift.

7. *Having difficulty loving.* Down deep, hopeless people lack faith in themselves. This inner emptiness and despair then gets projected outward to the whole world. If hopeless people seem short on love, it's usually because they feel they never got enough love at a crucial period in their lives. Of course, this is ultimately no excuse; plenty of love-deprived people have transcended their early affliction to become better, more compassionate people. But many hopeless people drive love away, either consciously or unconsciously.

What all of this really boils down to, of course, is fear. People tend to think of despair as the opposite of hope, but fear is probably hope's direct antithesis. In fact, fear is the basis of all other obstacles to hope. Destructive criticism is linked to the fear that others will find out that you're the one who isn't perfect. Dependence upon physical reality is rooted in a fear of the unknown, while buying into negative statistics is tied to fear of the known and fear that we don't have the power to change it. Belief in the virtues of suffering is really a fear of being happy; humorlessness is really the fear that others will be happy when you're not or that if you're too happy, you're sure to be punished sooner or later by the stern hand of fate. An inability to love results from the fear of not being worthy of love and of being rejected if we try to express love. And repressed emotion is simply the fear of loss of face, of letting loose, going crazy, being out of control, or being censured for our feelings. Fear is the great inhibitor of hope; it keeps our wings clipped and prevents us from believing in a future with meaning and purpose, which is what hope is.

So how do we counteract hopelessness and hopeless people?

The Seven Optimystic Antidotes to Hopelessness

1. *Humor.* The optimystic brings lightness and clarity to heavy and frustrating situations with the quality of compassionate humor. This is not insensitive laughter or humor at the expense of others, but a gentle, less serious way of viewing the world that lifts spirits and makes hope stir anew.

2. *Encouragement.* The optimystic is not out to criticize but to encourage. We all know that when people are criticized they become defensive, angry, and even despairing, and that when they are encouraged and applauded for their capabilities, they work harder and achieve more. The optimystic approaches people with the hopeful attitude that they can do better, they can achieve their goals and dreams, they can be happy, and, most important, they have the talents and tools within themselves to attain these things.

3. *Knowledge of the mystical reality.* The optimystic is always full of hope because she has experienced mystical reality: the world beyond the one visible to the naked eye. Mystical reality embraces all possibilities; it is a world where hope is a given because everything we could want or need, in the form of an eternal life force and union with God, already exists within us. Mystical reality urges us to find the still, sure voice within us that is our ever-present guide and help—our mystic self, which can tune in to new information and other dimensions at any time, in any place.

4. *Belief in the virtue of happiness.* The optimystic believes that being happy and making others happy is not only our right but our duty. The optimystic believes that good things are given to us for us to enjoy and that it would be basically rude of us not to appreciate them. Would we acknowledge a birthday gift by saying, "Gee, this is really nice, but I just can't accept it because how could I possibly deserve to be happy when the world is such a pit and other people are suffering? If I took your gift and enjoyed it, I'd be really selfish. So cram it!" Perhaps that's how God feels when we don't allow ourselves to experience happiness. When we don't allow ourselves to feel happy, we're likely to not allow others to feel happy either.

5. *Belief in miracles.* The optimystic knows that statistics are just markers, not absolutes. Therefore, we prefer to believe in miracles, which are

nothing more than alternative ways of approaching ominous situations in order to create the most positive outcome possible. If a statistic is not promising, the optimystic has hope in its larger significance; if, for instance, he becomes "a statistic" and loses his corporate job due to downsizing, he may say, "This is a perfect opportunity for me to do what I've always wanted to do—take a break, go on a spiritual retreat, let the universe guide me now." When faced with statistics, the optimystic never forgets Hope Rule #1: There is *always* hope.

6. *Freedom of expression.* Optimystics allow for the expression of emotions and feelings, which are the doorways to the spirit. They respect the creative power of emotions and are not afraid to journey with them into regions of the psyche, the unconscious, and the imagination that hold the answers to many difficulties and the keys to many joys. At the same time, an optimystic is not threatened by others' emotions or embarrassed by their feelings; instead, she helps them to explore and work with their feelings positively and productively, knowing that in this fertile ground of vulnerability and openness to change, the seed of hope can take root.

7. *Generosity with love.* Above all, the optimystic provides hope through love. If God is love, the optimystic can be a distributor, giving love without restrictions or fear. The optimystic also receives love with an open heart free of expectation or conditions. It is in an atmosphere of love, after all, that hope is supported and strengthened.

The Hopeful Power of Humor

We both feel that one of the greatest gifts each of us has been blessed with was growing up in a family where humor was regarded as essential and admirable. We were rewarded for bringing humor to the dinner table; during trying times, we saw the power laughter had to hold our families together and give them the strength to persevere. And, most important, we learned early that humor could raise the spiritual vibration in any situation.

The importance of humor lies not in its power to subjugate but in its power to disarm. In a tense situation, humor lightens the atmosphere, allowing people to see things differently—from a broader, less self-centered perspective. How can we really enjoy and appreciate this stage show called life if we can't laugh at its often ridiculous ironies? The primary role of humor is to liberate us from the misery of tunnel vision. It elevates us above the problem or cause of our pain. In many societies, humor has been the primary defense of the people against oppression.

In certain religions, humor is a defense against the oppression of illusion as well as a force to uplift the spirits of the world. Do you remember a time when you felt really down and a friend's funny story or comment brought you out of the doldrums? Or how about a time when you were able to raise someone else's spirits with a smile and a laugh? Humor is not just a superficial approach to life; it is the supreme balancing mechanism. It helps us to right ourselves when we feel like we're falling into darkness, to put things once again into their proper, balanced perspective so that we can acquire renewed energy to solve our problems and move ahead rather than become bogged down in sorrow and suffering. When we can laugh at our oppressors and our fears, we disempower them. This is why the spiritual warrior has a sense of humor and brings it to others as an instrument of peace and hope.

A good sense of humor indicates our readiness to embrace life. It is a cornerstone of health, both mental and physical. Many studies have proven that laughter is therapeutic, that the actual physical act of laughing improves circulation and oxygenation and boosts the immune system. A study done at New York University even showed that a day of fun strengthened the immune system for forty-eight hours afterward, whereas a day of sadness only depressed the immune system for twenty-four hours. It looks like the *Reader's Digest* had a handle on something when it coined the immortal phrase, "Laughter, the best medicine." Therefore, our optimystic good sense cautions us to beware of humorless people, because they have the noxious habit of killing hope and fostering despair, the real enemy of life.

There is a lovely story in the Talmud in which a rabbi stops the prophet Elijah in the marketplace and asks, "Is there anybody in this marketplace who will have a share in the world to come?" Elijah points to two men. When the rabbi asks their occupations, they reply, "We are merrymakers. When we see men troubled in mind we cheer them, and when we see two men quarreling we make peace between them." What could be more of a gift than the lightening of our burdens of worry, sadness, and anger? What could please God more?

Zen tales are forever poking fun at those who take enlightenment so seriously that in their frantic chase after it, they are constantly tripping over their own pomposity. As a result, they will never catch up with it—as if it could ever be caught up with in the first place. One of the more delightful illustrations of this is the story of an egotistical priest whose boring intellectual knowledge of Zen eventually drove his students toward the more heartfelt lectures of a simple Zen master. The jealous priest decided to confront the master and debate him. "Hey!" he hollered insolently. "Whoever respects you will obey what you say, but I don't respect you. So I dare you to make me obey you!"

"Come up beside me, and let's discuss it," said the master.

The priest bustled up to the master, bursting with his own self-importance.

"No, no, over here, on my left side," the master motioned to him. The priest moved to the left of the master.

"Actually, I think we can talk better if you're on my right," the master mused. So the priest moved over to the right side of the master.

"You see," said the master, "you are obeying me!"

In every society and culture there is the tradition of the trickster, the person or entity whose job is to remind us that if we should make the error of taking ourselves too seriously, watch out! The trickster is a true hero, a divinely inspired rebel whose gifts to us include the enlightened qualities of humility and grace, who forces us to remember who is really in charge, and who gives us the greatest enlightenment opportunity of all, the chance to laugh at ourselves and celebrate our wonderful, God-given imperfections. After all, no man is so perfect that he cannot laugh at himself. The trickster plays a particularly profound role in Native American stories, in the form of the wily Coyote, an inveterate mischief maker who can always be counted on, with his legendary cleverness, to cut us poor humans down to size. The most salient truth of enlightenment is that humanity is a bubble of self-importance, just begging to be burst. And there is God's heavenly messenger, the trickster, with pin poised in the air. The trouble is, we never know when he'll strike, which only adds to the fun. But the trickster is not just a humiliator; he is an inspiration, challenging us to seize life's opportunities and work the magic of imagination upon them, to enjoy the spontaneity, the unexpectedness of life, to let go of the need to possess all the answers, and to allow ourselves instead to become students of the moment.

"What's So Funny?" Find Out for Yourself

Is everyone born with the ability to sense humor? We would like to think so, because we feel that it is a divine gift that serves an important purpose in all of our lives. If you have not been skilled or trained in the art of humor, it is certainly not too late to start. Some people have a natural ability to make others laugh, and they have probably been doing it from a very young age. It's equally important to have the ability to appreciate humor.

We suggest that you start to take your own humor inventory. Get in the humor groove. Make a conscious effort to find humor in your daily activities. If you're always in the habit of taking things too seriously, slap yourself on the hand, let go of your worries, and just make yourself laugh at something. You might even want to be really daring and give yourself a full-blown giggle attack. If you've forgotten how to do it, take yourself back to the high school classroom, when something struck your funny bone at a most inopportune time. There you are, cracking up like a maniac, with everyone staring at you. "Would you like to share with the rest of us what you think is so funny?" your teacher icily inquires. Unfortunately, the stern chill in her voice only makes you laugh even harder, until the whole class is convulsed along with you. You know the scenario. Go for it! If such unbridled lightheartedness is a little too weird for you at first, start slowly and release your seriousness bit by bit. Sometimes we have to build up to an enlightened attitude a few minutes at a time, until we can actually sustain it for an hour, a day, the rest of our lives.

Or perhaps you're too serious because you're concerned with keeping up an image, while down deep you really are a riot. Are there things that crack you up that seem to be incongruous with the image you project or the way others expect you to be? There are probably a lot of closet humor addicts around who secretly like things that the "cool police" would give out tickets for. But optimystics know that being too cool is really hard work. We miss out on a lot of fun when we let ourselves go only to the movies the top critics approve of instead of bravely appearing in public and laughing ourselves silly at *Ernest Scared Stupid*. Optimystic warning sign: Beware of critics, who are not always the most humorous of creatures and who often enjoy puffing up their own egos at someone else's expense. When we put too much stock in the opinions of the critics, we risk being cheated out of some good laughs. And we cheat ourselves out of the fun of being ourselves when we care too much about what others think.

Bringing Up the Lights

"En-lightening up" helps us to see things more clearly. Enlightenment has been described as coming out of the darkness of illusion and misperception into the clear light of true awareness. When we cultivate lightness of spirit and heart, we move more quickly toward the light, and we also bring light to others.

To enlighten means to bring light to something, to bring a lighter perspective to a situation, to grow lighter in spirit. So the three essential aspects of enlightenment are clarity, humor, and lightness of being. Those who carry these items around in their optimystic toolbox are truly en-lightened.

Here are some good ways to en-lighten up:

1. Start noticing when you are having an attack of seriousness. Ask yourself, "What is so damn serious, anyway?" Pretend that you're looking at your problems through a close-up lens, and rate them on a Seriousness Scale of one to ten. Then, zoom out to a big wide-angle lens and view them in the larger context of the entire universe. What point value do they have now? Whenever you feel a seriousness attack coming on, counteract it as soon as possible with an absurdity attack, in which you allow the absurdity of the entire human condition to sink in. For instance, the real crackup is that we're in an impermanent world that we insist is permanent. That's pretty absurd, don't you think? When you can see your problems as ultimately impermanent and temporary, you can begin to en-lighten up.

2. Do something fun for somebody else. A woman we know has a wacky collection of off-the-wall cards and is always sending them to her friends, for no reason. She does it because it brings a moment or two of light into their lives when they least expect it. What other "random acts of lightness" can you think of that would bring up the lights in somebody's life?

3. Make a pact with yourself to spread laughter every day. This means either making others laugh or finding something to laugh at. We aren't talking about laughter at somebody slipping on a banana peel but rather joyous laughter, the kind that's good for both the human and cosmic systems.

4. Adjust your gratitude attitude. Sometimes when we are overwhelmed with seriousness we can en-lighten up the situation by taking inventory of the good things that might be happening to us at the same time but that sorrow, sadness, and anger often obscure from our view.

5. Do a give-away. Give away something to somebody who'd be grateful for it—not necessarily the junk in your basement, but something of value that you know a certain person or organization would appreciate.

Or begin divesting yourself of the stuff that might be tying you down. Remember: the lighter you travel, the more en-lightened you become.

6. If there is a trouble spot in your life, send light to it. Let go of all negative emotion connected to it, and simply surround the situation in light. Then spend some time meditating on the healing power of this light. Do this frequently, for a few minutes at a time. We guarantee that in a very short time you will "see the light" regarding your difficulty and will feel considerably freer and lighter about it.

10

Optimysticism Is Healthy Living

We focus our attention on everything that is far from our-
selves—the farther from our true selves, the more important we
think it is. We value our possessions and bodies above our minds,
our appearance above our health, our careers over our home life.
We accumulate possessions for our homes but do not take care of
our minds and bodies, although the most important conditions
for a home life are a happy mind and healthy body.

TULKU THONDUP RINPOCHE, *THE HEALING POWER OF MIND*

Optimysticism is a healthy style of life. Studies have consistently
shown that optimists live longer and maintain better health; the
Harvard School of Adult Development's extensive Thirty-Five-Year
Longitudinal Study on Optimism and Health, which ran from 1937
to 1965, followed ninety-nine Harvard graduates from the age of
twenty-five until the age of sixty. It was discovered that while the
subjects' health predictably worsened with age, "overall, men who
used optimistic explanations for bad events were healthier later in
life than men who offered pessimistic explanations." In further re-
search, psychologists Christopher Petersen and Linda Bossio reported, "Our studies all point to the same conclusion: optimistic
thinking is associated with good health, and pessimistic thinking is
associated with poor health."

In its combination of optimism and mysticism, optimysticism
naturally leads us in the direction of sound health because it urges

us to look for and create positive attitudes and outcomes. At the same time, it also promotes the spiritual serenity within us that allows us to make the important distinction between what we can control and what we can't. The issue of control is a major source of anxiety for many of us. We want desperately to be able to plan and orchestrate our lives so that we can live in the most stress-free, pain-free manner possible. Unfortunately, however, we sometimes don't have the final say in these matters, a fact of life that can, if we let it, disturb our entire equilibrium, both mental and physical. As we grow in our optimystic faith, however, we become more comfortable with letting go of the frantic need to control outcomes, because we have a deeper respect for the unknown, the mystery that is life. At the same time, we strive to open our minds, hearts, and imaginations to the realm of possibility rather than the realm of certainty. This way, we are more likely to be led to the right people and situations that will promote healing.

It is important to make the distinction between healing and curing. When we cure an illness, we eradicate its symptoms. But we may not be healing the body or the psyche in the process. Curing a disease, in the way of modern medicine, usually emphasizes symptoms rather than cause. Healing, on the other hand, is a state of mind, a state of equilibrium, that does not necessarily involve curing. Healing is a deeper approach to illness or imbalance; it seeks to get to the root of the problem, to find out why something occurred and how, through changing the cause, the outcome might be changed as well. One definition of *healing* is "making whole," and wholeness means that we honor the soul, the spirit, the body, and the mind as a unit. Thus, if the cause of a disease or difficulty cannot be altered, one can still be healed—made whole—through a change in attitude that involves the integration of the entire person.

The optimystic does not set out to dissect illness or cure but rather to ask the soul what the ultimate message is. Often healing is a matter of making peace with nonintegrated parts of ourselves, learning to truly love life, and accepting that regardless of circumstances, our lives can still be rich and purposeful. As optimystics, we know that we don't know everything and can't control everything; therefore, we appreciate the mystery and complexity of the concept of healing, honoring the process above the result. Above all, optimystics do not identify solely with the body; at the same time, they value the body as the vehicle through which the spirit and soul can do their work, and therefore they strive to create a healthy balance between the physical and the spiritual.

Balance Is Essential to Health and Healing

An ancient symbol of health and the healing profession is the caduceus, a winged staff entwined with two snakes, one white and one black, representing the balance of light and dark. The caduceus is the staff of Hermes and also of the archangel Raphael, who rules the spring, the time of year where there is a balance of daylight and night. Raphael's name translates as "the medicine of God," and his healing power comes from the establishing of balance.

Nature is a constant interplay of opposing forces that miraculously work in harmony. Sun and moon, winter and spring, yin and yang, feminine and masculine, right and left brain, negative and positive—all are examples of opposing forces that cannot exist without each other and that ultimately work together to create a vital experience of life. This is the law of the universe. When we fight this law, we create a war within us; when we accept our true nature, we live in peace and truth. So optimystics are not afraid to look at all the parts of their lives as necessary in order to effect the unity of the whole. They are disturbed not by darkness, but by imbalance.

Balancing Acts

In a way we are all tightrope artists, for our great task as physical and spiritual beings is to walk in the air while maintaining a firm footing on a solid base. In other words, keeping our spiritual and physical selves in balance is definitely an art as well as a strenuous, tenuous activity. The tightrope artist has a dual balancing act; he or she must be not only physically balanced, but also able to move effortlessly with total concentration. These techniques are essential for a healthy life as well. In order to have optimum health, our bodies must be balanced within themselves, all the parts functioning well. We must be in mental, physical, and spiritual harmony, with our thoughts and values in alignment with our actions.

The following is a list of acts of balance to help the optimystic coordinate behavior with ideals and feelings, which becomes the basis for mental and physical health.

1. *Act of balance: Aligning your behavior with your heart and mind.* We cannot ignore the fact that our behavior is what makes the most indelible impression on others and on the soul of the world. Our thoughts have power too, but how we put them into action matters the most. In the area of love, behavior is the most important component. We may feel love in our hearts and think that we are loving in our minds, but if we don't act lovingly, where is the love? Many people enter relationships before they are willing to behave lovingly toward their mate. They constantly seek proof of love instead of actually learning how to love. This is a tough balancing act. No one ever said a relationship is supposed to be easy; in fact, the greatest lessons in life come from the difficulties arising from human relationships. The optimystic is aware that love is a behavior, not just a feeling or a God-given right. It cannot exist until it is put into action.

2. *Act of balance: Aligning your behavior with your values.* Another area of difficulty that can lead to troublesome splits in our psyche is when our values do not correspond with our everyday actions. Too many of us, for instance, compromise our spiritual values when we make career decisions. This disparity stems from a skewed sense of what success is. The obvious measures of success in our society are monetary wealth, powerful professional position, and, of course, fame. The latter gets so out of hand that, in an effort

to distract ourselves from our own inner work, we blatantly engage in celebrity worship, only to be disillusioned or righteously indignant when our idol's all-too-human behavior spoils our fun.

As optimystics, however, we know that real success—of the spiritual variety—is measured by the degree of our ability to love and the degree of congruence between our values and our actions. Have you thought about your values lately? Take a moment to list your values (not your valuables). If you find that your list contains things like *family, friends, love, hope,* and *making a positive mark on the world,* then your values are spiritually inclined. Now take an honest look at this list and decide if you have compromised any of your values lately. Sometimes the compromises are hidden. For example, your job may demand that you promote something that pollutes the environment. While you may disapprove of this act, you may feel compelled to go along with it because you either have a family to support or a standard of living to uphold. You may believe that you're putting your family first by keeping your job, but the effect your compromising situation has on the bigger picture gets blurred. In other words, if you are helping to pollute the planet for a momentary gain, the long-term effect will actually damage the planet and you will not be doing any good at all for your family's future.

One subtle but powerful aspect of the business world is the tendency to tell "white" lies all day long. It's so easy to slip into this mode, from falsely flattering a client to pretending to be in a meeting to avoid people you don't want to talk to. You might not think of this behavior as lacking in integrity. You may even justify it as necessary or expected in your work; more sobering is the probability that you might even be commended by your superiors for playing the game so well. But the voice of truth doesn't like to be silenced, and the eventual result of a life lacking in personal integrity may be a compromise in your health, in the form of depression or illness.

Being conscious of our values is one of the healthiest things we can do for ourselves, because integrity has a miraculous way of taking the pressure off our spiritual nerves. How do the words *ethical, noble, moral, integrity, conscientious, scrupulous, upright,* and *decent* make you feel? If they make you feel good, pay attention, and if they make you feel judgmental, reflect upon how you may be projecting your own disappointment in yourself onto those people who seem to embody these virtues in every action of their lives. If you are presently in a situation in which you are compromising your values, regardless of what it entails, do something to change this. Pray for guidance; this is a critical issue concerning the health and well-being of your body and mind. Realize that integrity is the key to happiness; we cannot be happy if we are not true to ourselves, regardless of how many rewards we may receive for our behavior. Virtue, after all, is its own reward.

3. *Act of balance: Aligning your mental, emotional, and spiritual selves with your physical body.* The optimystic knows that we are spirits, temporarily housed on earth in the temple of the body. But many of us do not respect our bodies as sacred dwellings. Caught up in the pressures of daily life, our priorities quickly become misplaced. We strive to accomplish our goals; at the same time, we eat poorly, don't make time to exercise, or use drugs and alcohol to reduce the anxiety that our high-speed lifestyle is causing us. As optimystics, we are required to assess and correct this situation, because our bodies are the vehicles through which we accomplish the higher purpose of our mystic selves.

Healing is wholeness. We cannot be whole if our bodies are not in alignment with our psyches. When a body is whole—when all of its parts are synchronized—it is in balance. So, if you haven't been in the habit of paying attention to the needs of your body, it's time to do so. Optimysticism does not advocate neglecting the physical self for the joys of transcending the physical self. If you are not comfortable with or in your body, think about why and begin to take some actions to change your attitude. Realize that the fact that you are here means that you are supposed to be here. You're not flying around with the angels; you're not a dog or a tree. You are a human being who has specifically been given a physical body through which to fulfill your spiritual destiny.

4. *Act of balance: Realizing that finding balance is a continuous process.* We can't expect to remain fixed forever in a perfectly balanced state, simply because nothing in the universe ever stands still. Movement, not stasis, is the norm; therefore, as our situation or experience changes, we will always have to be taking rebalancing actions. In his lovely book *The Way of the Owl*, Frank Rivers observes,

> The curious thing about balance is that while it must be sought, it can never be achieved. If everything stayed still, achieving balance would be relatively easy. We could simply measure the excesses and deficiencies and even them out. But since the world is always in motion, balance can never be complete or final. Like birds in flight, we always have to adjust for new conditions.

We need to have a balanced perspective, then, on balance. We can't be disappointed or disillusioned if, after we've taken so much trouble to become balanced, the ground suddenly shifts beneath us. This is the way of the universe, after all. The ground is constantly shifting; why should we expect our lives on it to be any different? So remember that being in balance requires an attitude of openness to change and the cultivation of flexibility.

The Optimystic Chemistry Lab

Among the many mysteries of the human body, perhaps the most amazing one is that we are virtually little chemical factories. Our minds and bodies function by way of a multitude of chemical reactions; we respond to people according to the chemistry of our relationship with them. So when we feel engulfed by negative emotions, we can always go into the chemistry lab in our image-nation and do some alchemy.

Some universal base elements, for instance, perpetuate destruction. These elements are hatred, anger, jealousy, and greed. They spring from selfishness and the narrow thinking that we are not getting what we are entitled to. When these elements are present in our lives and consciousness, somewhere our body, mind, and spirit are being compromised and the seeds of sickness can germinate. Certainly anger can come from a valid place, but when we hold onto it or act out of our anger, we bring forth bad medicine that needs to be alchemically altered for the best. So, because these mind states can easily endanger the quality of life on Earth, they require a quick trip to the chemistry lab before they manifest in negative ways.

If you're consumed by worry, go into the lab in your mind. Then think of the base elements of worry and write them down. For example, worry over lack of money may contain the base elements of *fear* (that you won't have food and shelter), *anxiety* (that you will lose control over your life), and sadness (that you have lost your sense of security). So fear, anxiety, and sadness are the base elements that need to be transformed. What are the "alchemicals" you'll need to do this? Well, try adding a dose of *faith* to the situation. Faith automatically changes the chemical makeup of fear, for fear cannot exist in the presence of faith. In order to transform anxiety into inner peace, add a bit of *centering*. Take lots of deep breaths, go into your center, and feel your power, your sense of control, returning as you realize that while you may not be able to control every external event in your life, you do have complete control over whether or not these events overwhelm you. To counteract the sadness, add a generous amount of hope as well as descriptions of some hopeful scenarios that could change your situation in a positive way. Mix the whole brew up, and feel the contents transform as the chemical components are altered. You have neutralized fear with faith, anxiety with centeredness, sadness with hope. You should feel the shift from negative to positive charge.

As you return from the chemistry lab, remember to maintain the power of the alchemy by keeping the positive images in focus. After you have discovered what allows hope to flourish, go back to those images often to keep them alive—and always leave room for more alchemy and magic to take place.

Some Other Subjects for Lab Experiments

Stubbornness. Base elements: pride, laziness, passive-aggressiveness, stuck beliefs. Suggested remedy: humility, forward action, honesty, tolerance, openness, flexibility.

Guilt. Base elements: resentment, negative thinking, cowardice, low self-esteem. Suggested remedy: forgiveness, positive imagery, self-love, and respect.

Blaming. Base elements: puerile behavior, fear of your own success, self-pity, inertia, lack of imagination. Suggested remedy: taking responsibility, rethinking success, becoming busy enough to not have time to feel sorry for yourself.

Unhappiness. Base elements: depression or lack of energy, ungratefulness, disappointment, feeling like a victim. Suggested remedy: passion, gratitude, hope, self-love, centering.

Narcissism. Base elements: selfishness, egocentricity, denial, dissatisfaction. Suggested remedy: compassion, reality checking, contentment, Or, if all else fails, an all-expenses-paid vacation to Bosnia!

Mean-spiritedness. Base elements: anger, hatred, hoarding mentality, entitlement fantasies. Suggested remedy: loving-kindness, promoting loving behavior.

The universal optimystic rescue remedy for combating most enemies of exceptional mental peace is a synergistic combination of integrity, faith, patience, acceptance, humility, generosity, gratitude, wisdom, forgiveness, passion, and hope.

The Blessings of Contentment

One of the key reasons optimystics are healthier than the average person is that they are always finding new ways to be content.

Studies show that contentment is an essential component of mental peace and overall health. Dr. Dean Ornish, the physician who has become famous for his program of reversing heart disease without the use of drugs or surgery, observes in *Healing and the Mind,*

> Providing people with health information is important, but it's not usually enough to motivate lasting changes in behavior unless we also deal with the more social and even spiritual dimensions, and that's why I think it's so important to address those, as well as the behaviors. When people learn to experience inner peace—when we work on that level—then they are more likely to make and maintain lifestyle choices that are life-enhancing rather than self-destructive.

Think about where contentment gets you versus where dissatisfaction gets you. On the one hand, if we are contented with a bad situation because we have not set our sights high enough or have not remained true to our principles, it is better to be dissatisfied. But there is an important difference between true contentment and simply settling for less. True contentment is a function of our ability to live in the spiritual moment, the awe-inspiring present. When we are truly content, we are drawing from the moment, sustained by its remarkable life-affirming energy. We are so busy being in wonder, so busy absorbing the exciting possibilities for experiencing aliveness that the present affords us, that we don't have time to be discontent. As a result, we feel balanced, energized, and whole—the three most essential attributes of a healthy person.

Dissatisfaction, on the other hand, is useful only as an improvement tool. It can be a powerful energy source and impetus for change, but when it becomes a permanent outlook, the positive energy that it can generate *degenerates* into frustration, anxiety, and unhappiness. Understanding the natural law of opposing forces working to create synergy, an optimystic is aware of the need to balance contentment with dissatisfaction. If we feel dissatisfied with someone or something, what is this telling us? Are we being too picky, too negative? Or is this a message that we need to rebalance, to change a relationship or a situation? If dissatisfaction can propel us to contentment, fine; if, for instance, we discover spiritual satisfaction as a result of being unhappy with a life based solely on material achievement, then dissatisfaction is a true blessing. But if we are always dissatisfied, if contentment always seems to elude us, we need to take a good look at what beliefs and attitudes may be preventing us from pursuing a meaningful and happy life.

Signs of Contentment

1. You are so busy living that other people don't get on your nerves. You know how to live and let live. When the agitators show up, you are able to handle them quickly and artfully, by observing their behavior and choosing not to be around it.

2. You have sudden feelings of magnanimity for your fellow human creatures. A magnanimous person possesses the qualities of compassion and high-mindedness. When we are not content with life, we tend to expend more energy on ourselves and our petty problems than we do on others. When we are contented, however, we find that we have the time and the energy to be concerned about others, to treat them magnanimously.

3. Forgiveness is important to you. You can easily forgive the small irritations of life, and you have learned to take an objective view of the big ones. As a result, you can rise above any small-mindedness and begin to let go of resentment toward any harm that might have been done to you.

4. You respect yourself and are forgiving of your own faults, and you are careful not to let others rule you with the iron fist of guilt.

5. You feel sweet inside as opposed to bitter.

6. You know what it means to have a heart *full* of love.

For good mental and physical well-being, make contentment a regular practice in your life. Start the moment you wake up. When you awake, spend a few moments in gratitude. Think about the good things in your life and say them out loud. Even if they seem paltry, acknowledge them.

Begin to fully realize the value of good health. We often take our health for granted until it is too late. But just as contentment leads to good health, good health leads to contentment. Spend some time every day doing something healthy for yourself. This doesn't have to be a big thing; it can mean taking a fifteen-minute walk or getting a massage or setting aside some time for fun. But it is best as a daily practice, a continuous process.

Appreciation opens doors; ingratitude closes them. Do an inventory of your life. What do you really, truly appreciate? Where have you not been appreciative when you could have been? Think about the positive ways appreciation has influenced your life and the negative effects ingratitude has had. What can you begin appreciating more, right now? Remember that to *appreciate* means "to increase in value." When you appreciate people and experiences, you increase the value of those things in your life, and your life increases in value, to yourself and to others.

O11

Perfection: An Affront to God

Since everything is but an apparition,
perfect in being what it is,
having nothing to do with good or bad,
acceptance or rejection,
one may well burst out in laughter.

LONG CHEN-PA

Optimystics are not perfectionists. Why? Because perfection is, first of all, an illusion and, second of all, a trap. As soon as we believe in it, we are immediately prey to the antioptimystic forces of dissatisfaction and guilt. How can we be really content if we are always striving for perfection, when, as the true sage knows, nothing is perfect and everything is perfect? How can we rejoice in the moment and in ourselves when we are always feeling guilty, either consciously or unconsciously, about our imperfections?

The optimystic knows better than to go after perfection, because perfection is not something out there to be caught. We catch footballs and fish and diseases; we can't catch perfection. The great irony and paradox is that perfection doesn't, and does, exist. It *doesn't* exist in the form into which many religions and moral codes have perverted it—a single ideal of behavior and belief that is better than we are and that we must attain if we want to achieve sainthood or our eternal reward. It *does* exist, as the Buddhist mystic Long

Chen-Pa understood, in everything already, precisely as it is, because God, who is the only perfect one, created the world with all of its warts and nose hairs, and anything that comes from God must somehow be perfect, even in its imperfection.

In many cultures, the idea of attaining perfection is considered an affront to God, who is the only source of true perfection. An interesting cross-cultural phenomenon, for instance, is the purposeful creation of an imperfection in a work of art. Like the Amish quilters, who intentionally leave a flaw in their work, believing it to provide the space where God can come through most clearly, the Navajo Indians would put a mismatched color in their blankets, and Japanese tradition dictated that anything humanly made contain a tiny flaw so as not to insult God by presuming to be perfect.

There is the famous Zen story of the revered woman artist in Japan who was famed for making incense burners. Each burner was a work of art. Yet she was a total perfectionist who strove, throughout her life, to create the perfect incense burner. Finally, after years on this highly personal quest, she achieved what she thought was her goal, whereupon she took the burner and smashed it into a thousand pieces. The standard interpretation of this tale is that in striving for perfection, for enlightenment, we can never be satisfied with where we are, because enlightenment is not a destination but a perennial state of arrival. But other cultures might interpret this story differently, deciding that the artist had destroyed her perfect creation because to presume perfection is to one-up God.

Have you ever thought about the fact that perfection can actually inhibit growth? Perhaps the artist destroyed her burner because she realized that if she really had created the perfect work of art, she had no place left to go. The optimystic knows that it is the process, not the end result, that makes life exciting. How uninteresting the world and our relationships would be if we were perfect! Acknowledging our imperfections allows us to grow spiritually, opening doors to the Holy Spirit. God speaks to us most directly through our imperfections—through the failures and disappointments that lead to awareness, growth, and change, through the yearning place in our souls that seeks wholeness, union, peace. If we were perfect, after all, not only would we not need each other—we wouldn't need God. Or else, we would already be in perfect union with God, which is a state of heaven, not of earth.

The Insidious Trap of Perfection

Why do we have the word *perfect* if there is no such thing? When and where did the guilt trip of perfection begin? Why is perfection such a powerful illusion in our society? What is going on here?

Take the notion of the perfect body. For some strange reason our society perpetuates a belief that there actually is such a thing as a perfect body. The media bombards us so relentlessly with images of these perfect bodies that we become hopelessly hooked on what we aren't, and we begin looking all over for ways to correct the situation. So we join gyms that we never go to, we start diets that we never finish, we pay thousands to have face-lifts, butt-lifts, breast implants, nose jobs, and any kind of makeover that can transform us into what we are told is desirable. Yet it never, ever works, does it? We have fallen into the trap of perfection; we have climbed aboard the cycle not of life but of false hope and despair. And even more sadly, the "perfect" bodies we see gleaming at us from magazine covers and TV commercials often contain the emptiest and most despairing of psyches. How many famous models have we read about who were anorexic and miserable, who felt only as good as their latest weight, whose lives could be ruined in an instant by a pimple? Perhaps the most laughable illusion of all is the belief not only that there is a perfect body, but that it could last forever. When we fall for that one, we fall further into the perfection trap. Now, in addition to being eternally dissatisfied with our looks, we are terrified of losing them. So we begin running from age and death in some crazed belief that we can actually defy nature and thwart the inevitable. In our dogged pursuit of the false god of physical perfection, we deny ourselves any opportunity we might have for living fully, aging gracefully, and dying peacefully. We not only missed the ball; we missed the game.

Or how many times have you heard yourself or another complain about a present relationship while pining away for the perfect soul mate? We are forever looking for that significant other who will make us perfectly happy, solve all our problems, give us all the energy and love and reason for living that we could want. But it is only until we have grown very old and very wise, at which point we are probably beyond needing the perfect person, that we realize that he or she never existed except as a projection of our illusions. Why else do relationships fizzle and die; why else are marriages, potentially the most important and spiritual of unions, so incredibly difficult to sustain in a healthy, life-affirming way? Because we are expecting the other person to deliver us and to conform to our ideals in the process. In essence, we have married our own illusions.

But optimystics understand that each human is born with a unique way to express, give, and receive love, regardless of the package he or she comes in. All relationships are important for our growth. Perfection is most blatantly an affront to God when we continuously seek out a perfect person to reward with the prize of our love. There is no perfect time to give love; it is required of us in each and every moment. Perfection is a direct route out of the spiritual moment and into the ever-elusive future. If we expect it in our relationships, we will discover, to our regret, that in waiting for it to happen, we are denying ourselves the chance to experience it as it is, right now, right here.

The quest for perfection can destroy a perfectly good person. The quest for the perfect body causes some people to starve themselves to death. The craving for perfection can lead some to commit suicide when they feel like they have failed because something didn't go right and their idea of perfection is suddenly snatched away from them. There are many ways to cheat ourselves out of a meaningful, deep experience of life, and one sure way is to chase after some notion of perfection outside of ourselves. This has never proved to feed the soul, yet many people spend most of their energy doing anything it takes to find the perfect mate, job, family, life. Funny thing is, we rarely find people anxious to attain the perfect psyche and perfect inner harmony. Could it be because this requires us to go inside, instead of outside of ourselves, to a place where we really have to take responsibility for everything?

Most people would agree that their biggest fear in a relationship is not being accepted as they are, with all their faults. Or they may fear being rejected for *not living down to* another's expectations, for being their highest and best selves and in the process making the other person feel inadequate and resentful. When we reject others for what we perceive of as a fault in them, chances are very good that this fault looms large in our own psyche. Judging and criticizing, the stringent by-products of perfectionism, are good ways to ensure that we will never be happy, with ourselves or anyone else; they will always keep us focused on the illusion of superiority at someone else's expense, while we know, deep down in our souls, that our superiority is only a mask we put on to hide our real feelings of inferiority.

By accepting others' faults, however, we discover that we can accept ourselves. It's an old saying that what we dislike in others usually mirrors the same characteristic in us. Think about some people who really bug you. What is it about them that you find so annoying, so unacceptable? Are they self-centered? Pompous? Are they always doing dumb things that get them into jams? Make a list of some of the things about other people that really push your buttons. Now look honestly at yourself. What are some of your own little imperfections that might drive other people up the wall? Is there any congruence between the two? Take a moment now to accept yourself, faults and all. Say to yourself, "I'm human. I've got good and not-so-good qualities, just like everybody else. I accept the fact of my humanness and the humanness of others, while being open to changing the aspects of my personality that might cause me to devalue my worth and the worth of others."

The acceptance of imperfection can thus work miracles in our psyches and lives, freeing us to love without fear of rejection, to explore without fear of disappointment, to create without fear of failure. This is why the optimystic sees imperfection as a blessing; it is the most direct route to our vulnerability, which is not our weak spot, our Achilles' heel, but rather the open space in our heart that lets God in.

Sensing Beauty

Human beings have long lived in the shadow of the ideal of perfect beauty, not realizing that beauty is a divine healing force that has nothing to do with perfection. If perfection is the goal in creating beauty, the attempt will be thwarted and all that will remain will be a sterile image with no true soul. The maker of the incense burner searched for beauty, only to destroy it when she found it. But perhaps if she had been able to see the beauty in everything she did, all of her creations would have been masterpieces.

How do we know when we are in the presence of beauty? If beauty is judged only by the eye, without the input of the heart, the reading is always suspect. How does a blind person know when she or he is in the presence of beauty? By the *feel* of it. Blind people use all of their other senses to compensate for sight. They will feel someone's face and know it as intimately as those who can see it. Their hearing may be far more acute than the seeing person; they may pick up on the vibrations of music or the subtleties of the voice or the real intent behind words in a way that makes the average person seem deaf by comparison. Their sixth sense of intuition may be always tuned in. So beauty is not an external phenomenon but rather an internal experience judged by its essence, not its appearance.

Interestingly, optimystics become blind to external measures of beauty as their third or mystic eye is opened—the most accurate organ of vision when it comes to seeing true beauty. It's the oldest of truths that we see and exude beauty through the light within us. A work of art touches our soul; a person who is not attractive in the classic sense or who might even be called ugly by society's standards of desirability may nonetheless be regarded as beautiful because of the irresistible beauty of soul light that shines through in everything this person does. The optimystic has no preconceptions about beauty, knowing that to judge things by external criteria of beauty is to blind oneself to the hidden and unexpected beauty that is all around us. When we get to the point of knowing where our own beauty comes from and can rest assured that we are physically, soulfully, and spiritually beautiful, we will take beauty with us wherever we go. And, most important, we will be able to see the real beauty in others.

Divine Artistry

Art is the Holy Spirit breathing through your soul.
                                                      Jack Kerouac

Spiritual creativity is the physical expression of our love and of our deepest connection to life. Perfectionism can easily silence our creativity, for it is the motivation behind criticism, which, if used destructively, kills hope and confidence. "Works of art," wrote the poet Rainer Maria Rilke, "are of an infinite solitude, and no means of approach is so useless as criticism. Only love can touch and hold them and be fair to them." Optimystics strive to stay aligned with what brings meaning and beauty to life. If the critics agree, fine. If not, it's too bad that they're blind to something the optimystic finds inspiring. The way of the heart, where creativity resides, is not open to debate. It is a uniquely personal response to life, just as optimysticism is ultimately a uniquely individual experiment in divine creativity.

Divine creativity is the way in which we call God into our lives by creating something from the heart, from the center of our love. What we create does not have to be tangible. We can create beautiful moments and transform ordinary things when we imbue them with love. Many people who have a loving relationship with themselves and God create an atmosphere of peace and joy. Others may inspire people by their compassion, creating divine moments of hope wherever they go. In Zen Buddhism, the idea of art and creativity centers around the union of the artist and the moment. The true artist works only with what is there at the moment of creation, acting as an open vessel, an unobstructed channel free of preconceptions and expectations.

Hildegarde of Bingen, a famous Christian mystic born nine hundred years ago who left an amazingly versatile legacy of art, music, plays, and other writing, had a lot to say about divine creativity. Hildegarde spent her first forty-two years denying her creativity-centered spiritual experience. Once she owned it, however, she spent the rest of her life, until her death at age eighty-three, painting, writing, composing, healing, preaching, founding, organizing, letter writing—in short, making sure she shared her creative images and visions in any way she could find. She declared, "Humankind alone is called to co-create. We should be the banner of Divinity; God created humankind so that humankind might cultivate the earthly and thereby create the heavenly."

Hildegarde felt that "drying up" was a sin that happened when you ignored "greening power" (creative energy) and stopped creating. A sure way to dry up is to torment yourself with perfection, to not create for fear of not attaining perfection, or to create for another's approval rather than one's own. Even though she later was canonized, Hildegarde knew better than anyone that divine creativity is not the province of the saint or the genius; it is the birthright of every human being. Too many of us have been conditioned to distrust our creative impulses or to believe that we just aren't the creative type. But this is a fallacy to be dismantled immediately. We are all creative because we are all creatures—creators—of God. Children are naturally, spontaneously creative, playing with any material at hand and transforming it into something new. It is only when they are taught perfectionism, when they are informed that their present creative efforts aren't good enough, that they begin to withdraw their creative impulses and limit their concept of self. Since we were all once children, it follows that we all have a natural compulsion to create. It may take some time to rediscover it, but if we don't honor it we may create problems for ourselves, which will be unsatisfactory substitutes for creative expression. It is the suppressing and stifling of the divine creativity within us that leads to everything from illness to madness. As Jungian analyst Robert Johnson observes, "When we don't go to spirit, spirit comes to us, in the form of neurosis." The optimystic is actively inspired to heights of divine creativity because his or her creative efforts are not made for the praise of the critics, but in praise of God. So perfectionism cannot intrude, because whatever we offer up to God is perfect in God's eyes.

Letting Go of Perfectionism

Imagine being content with an imperfect self. This is a what-if game:

★ What if you were born autistic? Should you be denied happiness in life because you can't express yourself? Does your silence mean you aren't thinking, feeling, appreciating? How does anyone else know what's in your head, your heart, your soul? How can we respect the different realities that our fellow humans experience? We can't if there's a universal yardstick by which we measure perfection.

★ What if you could celebrate your imperfection? How would you go about doing it?

★ What if you began appreciating imperfections in others as affirmations of their humanness? What if you stopped trying to change someone close to you and accepted that person for exactly what she or he is? How would this change the relationship you have with this person?

★ How many areas of imperfection can you recognize in your life? Why do you think of them as imperfections? Is your standard of imperfection based on the opinions and beliefs of others or the sincere desire within yourself to make a change? What if you accepted these imperfections and decided that you are going to learn from them rather than run from them, deny them, or try to change them without first understanding them?

★ What if you let yourself create a work of art without any expectations whatsoever, just letting the work emerge and reveal itself to you?

★ What if you wrote a bad poem?

★ What if you let go of any "ism" you have been labeling yourself with and found a new way to look at your own identity?

★ What if you were content with yourself as just who you are right now?

Ask Not What Life Can Do for You; Ask What You Can Do for Life

Business, then, clearly touches on many matters of genuine importance to the soul, but how is it involved with enchantment, and can there be such a thing as enchanted work and enchanted commercialism? One way to imagine enchanted business is to examine several aspects of business life and determine how they might have soul, how they might stir fantasy and increase the interchange between the life of things and the life of humans.

THOMAS MOORE, *THE RE-ENCHANTMENT OF EVERYDAY*

Many of us are used to thinking about life as a game that, if played well, drops a big jackpot into our laps. We expect life to give to us, in the form of money, success, happiness, security. But optimystics are more concerned with what they can do *for* life. They ask: How do I become more attuned to the bigger picture, to the world and God, of which I am an inexorable and therefore invaluable part? How do I heal feelings of separateness? How do I know when my heart is in my work?

These days people are talking more and more about how they want to simplify their lives. Often what they mean is that they would like to change the way they work. As optimystics, we want our work and our lives to be for a higher purpose. This may seem difficult, but it is mostly a matter of changing the way we think about work and changing little things in our life to make work more of an expression of ourselves.

How Does One Know One Is Being Called?

We are *all* being called. The very fact of our being put here on this Earth means that there was a reason for our existence and therefore a spiritual destiny that we are encouraged to fulfill. Our calling, our special human mission, is about what we *do* for life—how we live out our soul's purpose, how we translate the unique gifts we have each been given into a life of purposeful action. Having a calling can be a very simple and humble way of life. It does not have to mean we are hearing voices and leading armies into battle against the bad guys. But it does have to fulfill us, on a deeper level than mere material satisfaction.

What is the difference between our work and our calling? Most of us do something for a living, meaning we work at a job to make some money to pay for the things that are necessary for our comfort and survival. But as we all know, a job can be very different from what we perceive our life's work to be, especially if the work that gives us joy doesn't have a high salary attached to it. In his book *The Reinvention of Work,* Matthew Fox explores this difference: "Under the pressure of the world economic crunch that is creating a worldwide depression, the grave danger looms that we will seek only jobs—jobs at any price—and ignore the deeper questions of work such as how, why, and for whom we do our work."

What would you do if you really needed money and the only job available was cutting down trees in a rainforest? What if someone offered you three times the amount of money you were making now to do something intrinsically distasteful to you? Would it be an easy choice to make if you were offered a job at half your current pay that involved the real work you have been wanting to do? These may seem like simplistic questions, but the fact is that many of us today are in difficult financial predicaments that sometimes force us to turn a blind eye to our moral, ethical, and spiritual needs and obligations. As optimystics, we have to be willing to reexamine our priorities and unwilling to do things we don't believe in. This is often a question of trusting that our right and proper work will be given to us and will support us. In our hearts we know that any form of greed adversely affects the world's delicate ecological balance. But when our work is in alignment with our higher purpose, we are helping to maintain that balance.

Living a Spirit-full Life

Stop and think for a moment about some preconceptions you have about the word *spiritual*. What, exactly, does it mean? Write down some concepts or images that immediately come to mind. Your list might look something like this:

> Peaceful
>
> Kind
>
> Believing in God
>
> Unconditionally loving
>
> Centered

These may be attributes associated with the spiritual person. But what *spiritual* at its most basic means is to be spirit-full, filled with the spirit. And the spirit is the creative aspect of our being, the breath that awakens us to life. The word *inspiration* actually means "to breathe in." Thus to inspire, which means to excite or uplift us to achievement, means to be linked to the breath, the life force. This is why breathing is the first and most essential aspect of meditation. According to a yogic proverb, "Life is in the breath. Therefore, he who only half breathes, half lives."

Spirit, then, is life. It is also traditionally associated with fire, a purifying, illuminating element with tremendous power to create or destroy. Throughout history, in different cultures and religions, fire has been an image associated with the spirit. The Holy Spirit—the infusion of the spirit of God into humanity—is depicted as a flame.

One of Christianity's most powerful mystics, St. John of the Cross, wrote that he was guided only by his heart, which he referred to as "the fire, the fire inside!" We get "all fired up" when we're inspired. We refer to past loves as "old flames." The gifts of the spirit are passion, creativity, love, and renewal, all of which are symbolized by fire. So a spiritual person is, technically, a "spirited" person, one who is in sync with the life force, who is impassioned, creative, full of the spirit. Similarly, the great mystics, who were so imbued with the spirit of God, were people of great passion, who lived and breathed the life of the spirit in all of their daily actions. They were not merely ascetics who removed themselves from this poor old "vale of tears" as they eagerly awaited redemption; they were active participants in earthly life, which to them was a fascinating mystery as well as a gift to be experienced to the fullest.

Yet most of us never stop to think about our spirit and how it is functioning in our lives. If we are merely doing a job instead of working for life, we may be out of touch with the needs of our spirit, the messages it is trying to convey to us. As a result, we may not be answering the call of our passion, the avenue through which we can fully express our creative spirit.

Write down the answers to the following questions. How deeply are you in contact with your spirit? How effectively are you using the gifts of the spirit in your life? Is your work a source of creativity, passion, love? If not, why not? What would you *really* like to be doing? What fears may be holding you back from doing what your heart, soul, and spirit are calling you to do?

Are You Happy?

Very few of us can respond with an outright yes when asked if we're happy, because we have no idea what real happiness is. Happiness on the physical plane is almost always dependent upon circumstances, which are always changing. To humans, happiness and grasping go hand in hand. We cling to past memories of happiness, or to our current source of happiness, with nails firmly dug in. In this limited state of consciousness, the idea of letting go becomes synonymous with loss. We do not understand, until we begin living optimystically, that real happiness is, first of all, simply being able to appreciate what is. When we can not only want what we have but release what we have, knowing that we have only created a space for something new to come in, we know that we're listening to our mystic self.

Happiness also comes to us when we are doing our best for life. When we have discovered the work or activity that makes us feel excited, productive, and useful, we are much more inclined toward living a simpler life. We seem to need and want less when our work is so filled with spirit that we feel filled up.

Happiness is important for living a spirit-full life. When we present ourselves to the world in a truly happy state, we attract magic to us and encourage others to live according to the needs of their spirits. A happy state does not mean careening over the top with giddiness. Happiness is a beautiful way of being that allows us to sparkle with peace. When we are happy, we smile at the world and we take the time to enjoy our surroundings. We lighten up the atmosphere; we radiate a positive vibration to which others are automatically attracted.

Most people are unhappy because they think there is something out there that they have yet to find that will be the missing piece in their happiness puzzle. But the only missing piece is the awareness that happiness is a function of attitude, a state that can be attained in the twinkling of an imagination shift. As Dostoyevsky said, "Man is unhappy because he doesn't know he is happy."

The sad truth is that most unhappy people, the ones who let us know they are unhappy, usually are pouting because they're not getting their way. They focus on what is lacking instead of on the beauty each moment can bring us. Some of us look for a relationship to bring us the happiness we have been missing; others believe that money will buy us happiness, in the form of material comfort or the freedom to do whatever we want. But optimystics know that genuine happiness is a self-created experience that no one else can give us and that the key to happiness lies in our ability to transform everyday moments into spiritual ones.

Next time you go out, try to find someone who seems happy. Then, realize that you have no idea what that person has just gone through or how many trying lessons she or he is facing at the moment. It is an interesting phenomenon of human existence that the happiest people are often the ones who have survived incredible sorrow and tragedy and who have come through their experience with a deeper appreciation for everything, a deeper commitment to experiencing joy and meaning in their work and lives. Anne Frank once said, "Whoever is happy will make others happy too. He who has courage and faith will never perish in misery!"

If you aren't happy, what do you think is missing in your life? What has left a gaping hole in your happiness bag? Is it something you think you need but really don't? Or is it something more profound, like the calling that you haven't yet found? Ask yourself, "How can I make myself happy in spirit? What are the activities that will satisfy my deeper needs?"

Now, how can you begin to address those needs? Could you take a risk or two that you've been avoiding? Do you need to create more time in your life in order to do the thing that will ignite the flame of your spirit and bring you joy? Do you need to listen more to your intuition?

Our lives often change through what might be considered events of chance or coincidence. Our mystic selves are attuned to the kinds of synchronicities and unexpected events that so often alter our destiny. People may suddenly appear in our lives, bringing the guidance or help we've been looking for. We might be inexplicably led to a book that uncannily pertains to something we've been thinking about. When we make the decision to follow our spirits, we seem to become more attuned to divine instruction and more aware of divine help. Such messages and messengers may become regular occurrences in our lives—*as long as we are open to them.*

Finding Your Bliss

We've been encouraged by many gurus of the age to "follow your bliss." But you can't follow your bliss until you've figured out what it is. Sometimes we just don't know what it is that will make us truly happy or what our life's work is supposed to be. How do we find out?

We can suggest some things that will help you connect on a deeper level to your passion and your spiritual desires and integrate them more fully into your life.

1. *Practice expanding your vision.* As we saw in chapter 1, the word *vision* has many meanings. It refers to our dreams, goals, ambitions, and higher purpose. It represents the ability to see realms above and beyond tangible dimensions. Visionaries are people who see into the future, into what might be. People who have religious visions often receive mystical insight. In order to discover your bliss, visualize yourself in various situations in which you have been excited, happy, and energized. Note the common denominators of those experiences. Did they involve working with people? Working in the arts? The sciences? Did they fulfill some sort of creative need or use a talent? Now, expand your vision into the future. See yourself in some sort of work that involves your passion and is making you feel excited and uplifted. Is there anything—attitudes, beliefs, prejudices, fears—that might be clouding your vision and preventing you from actualizing your deepest desires?

In Native American culture, a vision quest is a pivotal journey into the deepest recesses of the self in order to discover one's spiritual destiny. This is a serious, rigorous undertaking involving various purification rituals, and when practiced correctly it leads to a mystical, transcendent, life-altering experience. While a bona fide traditional vision quest may not be practical for you, you might want to try a modified version, in which you set aside some time, preferably an entire day but at least a few hours, to go to a quiet place, do some of the meditation exercises suggested in chapter 3, and go deeply into your spirit, asking it for guidance and direction.

Focus on your higher purpose; ask it to reveal itself to you. Record any dialogues, messages, or insights you receive.

2. *Listen to your dreams.* Like *vision,* the word *dream* is significant on a number of levels. It is an experience we have while asleep, but it is also a vision we carry within us of how we would like things to be. Dream images are messages from our unconscious that can alert us to important aspects of our lives that we might otherwise ignore. When we become skillful at listening to our dreams, we often find answers to our conscious dilemmas.

The optimystic is a talented dreamer, working creatively with dreams to expand awareness and vision. Before you go to bed, practice concentrating on your higher purpose, your spiritual destiny. Say out loud, "Tonight I will dream about my higher purpose, my life's work. I will remember my dream and will awaken with deeper insight into this issue." It will probably take a while, but if you say this every night, you will eventually have your dream. Record any information you receive in your dreams. At the same time, pay attention to your daydreams, which are often much more than mere flights of fancy; they may indicate where your spirit and soul are the happiest.

3. *Ask for guidance.* Optimystics have a loving relationship with a higher power, however they perceive it. They are not afraid or ashamed to ask for divine guidance. Whenever you're feeling the need for assistance and clarity in your life, just ask for it. Put out an SOS to your mystic self, to God, to the angels, whoever. Then be patient, which means waiting in faith. Your call *will* be answered.

Creating an Optimystic Work Environment

Sometimes we can't just up and quit our jobs in order to follow our bliss. So the next best thing is to make the most of the work that we're doing. Work is perhaps the best opportunity for us to bring optimysticism into daily practice—to live in the spiritual moment and encourage others to do the same. The following ideas for creating an optimystic work environment are optional; any resemblance to a belief system is unintended.

1. *Get yourself in the optimystic frame of mind.* The environment you create begins the moment you wake up in the morning. So do something nice for yourself before you head out the door. Make sure you have a few moments of reflection and time to enjoy a special cup of coffee or tea. Offer a prayer for the day. If you really want to make a difference in your daily life, wake up and write for five to twenty minutes. We're not talking about the great American novel here; simply have a special journal on hand to record thoughts about your life, notes on inspiration from books you are reading, dream images that came to you in the night, and so on. If you think that you don't have time for this, sacrifice a half hour of your sleep time. You'll be surprised and delighted at the payoff.

2. *Know the difference between ambition and aspiration.* Ambition is a strong desire to achieve something and often creates a climate for manipulation. Aspiration, on the other hand, means aiming high while allowing for the highest good to come about. Louisa May Alcott said, "Far away, there in the sunshine are my highest aspirations. I may not reach them, but I can look up and see their beauty, believe in them, and try to follow where they lead." Ambition is often motivated by the ego; aspirations come from the higher self and do not carry with them the constraints of drive, manipulation, and impatience that often accompany an ambition. Become conscious of your aspirations, and keep yourself focused on them.

3. *Think about your workplace.* What have you done to make it your own? Is it beautiful? Does it represent your essence? We can use our creative spirituality to find beauty and imbue our surroundings with color and harmony. Read a book on feng shui, the Chinese art of placement, and design your office to be in harmony with the chi flow. Put fresh flowers on your desk, and bring them in to your co-workers. Put beautiful art on the walls. Use your imagination; it won't let you down!

4. *En-lighten up the atmosphere.* Bring humor and lightness of spirit to your interactions with others. Wear something silly once in a while, especially if it would be considered out of the ordinary for your personality. Encourage others to see the humor in situations. One woman we know who was working in a tense university office situation fraught with power struggles and job insecurity began a clandestine satirical newsletter about the situation. Soon everyone was laughing so hard that the stress in the office was instantly reduced. As one co-worker put it, "When you can laugh at the situation, it doesn't have power over you anymore."

5. *Turn the daily grind into daily bread for the soul.* Make work moments into spiritual moments. Think of struggles and frustrations as positive creative energy that will keep you going until the challenge is met. Allow your imagination room to soar. Take creative thinking breaks once an hour. Encourage others to talk about their spiritual goals and desires. You might even think about taking a fifteen-minute meditation break with your co-workers.

6. *Let go of perfectionistic expectations of yourself and others.* When other people start getting to you, see the situation as an exercise in letting go and in strengthening your resolve and tolerance. Try to see things from another's perspective. Learn to look at situations from a variety of angles, and don't get stuck on one viewpoint. Remember that nothing is *that* serious.

7. *Take an optimystic lunch break.* Do something special and out of the ordinary at lunchtime at least once a week. Visit a museum. Go to a favorite bookstore. Walk around the block and really notice where you are and who you are walking by. Look for secret agents— angels posing as people or mystics hiding behind the facade of the ordinary.

8. *Take a mental vacation.* Take five-minute mental vacation breaks at least once an hour. When you take a break, notice where your tension is, how you are sitting and breathing. Is the weight of the world on you? If so, where is it the heaviest? What does your soul want you to know? Check in with your heart's answering machine every once in a while. There might be a message.

9. *Be empathetic, be encouraging, but don't be pessimistic.* Often we try to prepare ourselves for disappointment, even if it isn't destined to happen, by being a pessimist just in case. Human beings tend to be pretty adept at pessimism because life often *is* disappointing. But as optimystics, it's our job to stay in the realm of optimism. When others around you are down or despairing, give hope and encouragement in any way that you can. Don't get swept along on the pessimistic rapids. Your positive energy will raise the vibrations around you and can do much to improve your work environment.

10. *Know when to stop working.* Too many of us become consumed by our work, staying late at the office or taking it home with us. If we work at home, it can be that much harder to get out of the work mode. When we become slaves to our work and don't allow ourselves time for fun, inner work, or relationships, we're working against our optimystic natures. Make sure you know when quittin' time is, and observe it every day. Nurturing our personal lives, and the others in it, should always be our number one priority.

Are You Due for a Spiritual Oil Change?

Ask a good question and you will find an intelligent answer. We started out this chapter with the question "What can we do for life?" We gave you some suggestions, but now it's your turn to ask yourself some good questions of your own. Here are a few to get you started. Take an hour out of your busy schedule and journal about them. You may be surprised by your answers.

1. For whom are you working?

2. For what are you working? A car, a house, a life, or for the joy of following bliss?

3. What do you think you came to this earth to do?

4. Where have you been?

5. Where are you at present?

6. Where are you going and why?

7. What are the deeper needs underlying your ambitions?

8. What are the fears that are keeping you from taking your rightful place in the world?

9. As an optimystic, where might you venture that you have never dared to venture before?

13

Blessed Are They Who
Do Not Depend on Luck

*True luck consists not in holding the best of the cards at the
table; luckiest is he who knows just when to rise and go home.*

JOHN MILTON HAY

The stronger we become in our optimystic outlook, the stranger
the concept of luck becomes. What, after all, is the traditional
definition of *luck*? Something fortunate that happens *to* us, not *because of* us. Lucky people win all the door prizes; the odds are in
their favor. To the optimystic, however, a belief in the odds is odd
indeed. Who in their right mind would want to relinquish the wondrous gift of human choice to the merciless master of superstition
or the capricious, random beneficence of luck or fate? We all have
the power within us to leave the table; why would we sit there
gambling with Lady Luck? Because until we really experience the
benefits of the responsibilities that go along with accepting the optimystic life, we will pursue what seems like the easy way out. And
on the surface, it seems much easier to play the victim, to blame
our misfortunes on bad luck, than it is to take full ownership of our
lives and our attitudes.

But victimhood has its own dear price. In return for the favor of
not having to make the hard decisions, we give up our chance to

create our own happiness. It's interesting to note that studies on human behavior show, time and again, that luck actually belongs to the domain of the pessimist. The distinguishing characteristic of the pessimist is a lack of hope, stemming from a feeling of helplessness. Essentially, the pessimist believes that events control his or her life. So it's not surprising that pessimists link "good" events to good luck, and "bad" events to bad luck. Optimists, on the other hand, tend to ascribe their successes to their own talents or decision-making abilities. Luck has no place in the optimist's worldview; attitude, effort, and personal choice, however, do. Optimists seem to understand the curious fact of life that the more energy we put out, particularly in the form of good old-fashioned work, the more luck we seem to have. In other words, how can our ships come in if we never take the time to send them out?

Blessings in Disguise

As optimystics, we would never want to limit an experience with the label of good or bad luck, since we're well aware that some of the worst luck often brings the greatest blessings. In fact, the adjective *blessed* is much more appropriate than *lucky* when it comes to describing the optimystic attitude toward good fortune. *Blessed* means we have an attitude of gratitude. When we are really blessed we want what we have; there is nothing we are chasing after to fix our lives. And similarly, when we are truly blessed we possess what the Buddhists refer to as the quality of equanimity, the ability to accept all events, happy or not, without judgment, as valuable and perfect parts of the whole. Who can be luckier than the person to whom "Pleasure-pain, praise and blame, fame and shame, loss and gain are all the same"? Such a person has been freed from the stranglehold of suffering.

Here's a great Chinese fable, which you may have heard before but which is always worth repeating. A farmer's prize horse was stolen. His neighbor came over to commiserate with him on his bad luck. But the farmer refused to make any judgments. "Who knows what is good and what is bad?" he mused. The following day a herd of wild horses came into his field, and he caught them. Again his neighbor came bustling over, this time to congratulate him on his good fortune. But all the farmer said was, "Who knows what is good and what is bad?"

The next day the farmer's son tried to mount one of the horses and broke his leg. Along came the neighbor, to offer his sympathy. The farmer, ever imperturbable, answered him with the same refrain: "Who knows . . . ?" And the next day the military came riding through, to conscript all young men for service, and, you guessed it, the farmer's son was spared because of his broken leg.

The farmer, of course, is the ultimate optimystic. Not only does he refuse to play the luck game; he accepts all that occurs with the equanimity born of mystic certainty. The farmer, the man of the earth, is also a sage, the man of heaven; he rests secure in the knowledge of the ultimate unity in all things. Life to him is a natural cycle of causes and effects, none of which can be labeled either good or bad, because neither can exist without the other. This story reminds us of the power of time and the willingness to wait things out; luck comes to the patient, not to the hasty. Accepting that cycles are an inevitable part of life brings us a new perspective on luck. Patience and delayed gratification, however difficult they may be to practice, are often the magnets that attract wonderful outcomes. When we are willing to wait for something to happen for us, we give divine providence a chance to go to work for us. When we allow things to happen in their own time, the outcome is invariably in our favor.

Feeling blessed rather than lucky allows us to be in the spiritual flow, in alignment with the natural laws of the universe. If luck happens *to* us, blessings happen by virtue of an attitude shift on our parts. If, like the farmer, we can shift from a belief in good and bad, desirable and undesirable, to one in which all events are greeted with equanimous curiosity, the blessing of detachment is our inevitable reward. And the further along we travel on the bodhisattva path, cultivating other actions and attitudes that promote our spiritual well-being and the spiritual well-being of others, the more blessed we will be.

Feeling Blessed

Optimystics feel blessed when:

- ★ We do not have to compromise ourselves; we live in integrity with our goals and our values.

- ★ We understand that love is an active behavior, not a passive energy, and that to be "in love" means to be in a state of participation in the growth, happiness, and illumination of others.

- ★ We realize inner peace, the peace that surpasses all understanding.

- ★ We can live in the world without taking it personally; we can respond to uncomfortable or hurtful situations compassionately rather than defensively.

- ★ We realize that anger is creative energy that can be channeled productively rather than destructively.

- ★ We are able to choose the path of forgiveness rather than hatred.

- ★ We can view other human beings from the mountain of acceptance rather than from the pit of judgment, understanding that each of us has a unique purpose with unique soul lessons.

- ★ We wake up feeling great and grateful.

- ★ We see aging as a beautiful natural process and death as rebirth.

- ★ We know that we can always call upon the sacred gift of humor to change the chemistry of any situation.

- ★ We delight in the fact that the more good fortune we wish on others, and the happier we are for the success of others, the more good fortune and success will flow into our lives.

- ★ We know that the *chance* for good fortune exists in each moment; all we have to do is claim it.

Luck and Superstition

Who or what determines the flow of luck in our lives? Is it the god Jupiter, the lord of luck? Is it a four-leaf clover or a rabbit's foot? Is it a novena to St. Jude? Is it the lines in our palm? Is it the position of the sun, the moon, the planets, the stars?

Symbols and predictors of luck have always intrigued human beings; it would be the rare one among us who wasn't tempted at some time or another to wear a lucky charm, pray for good fortune, take a swig of Love Potion Number Nine, or consult a horoscope for advice on what to do, when to do it, and who to do it with. But the fact of the matter is that the ruling element behind all belief in these luck devices is superstition. And the motivating element behind superstition is always fear. We do not believe in the positive aspect of luck so much as we fear the future, with all its dreaded unknowns. So we'll do anything to try to assure that the future is safe and comfortable and that, as far as possible, we'll be spared the terrible inconvenience of change.

For all our sophistication and jaded cynicism, we are, at heart, a woefully superstitious society. There is no better proof of this than the "Psychic Hot Line" phenomenon that's recently taken the airwaves by storm. "Luck is on the way because a psychic I paid three hundred dollars to said so!" Then there's the eternal phenomenon of the chain letter. You know the score: an unsigned photocopied message arrives in your mail, instructing you to send out twenty copies of this letter within seventy-two hours. If you do, you'll get the pot of gold at the end of the rainbow within a week, guaranteed. If you don't, your fate will be worse than Job's. Mrs. Carmella S. sent out this letter just as she was told, and she won six million trillion dollars two days later. But Mr. Horace D., who threw the letter in the trash, contracted the bubonic plague, and he and his whole family dropped dead within forty-eight hours.

Chain letters are designed to get you to do something superstitious through seduction and intimidation. If you're human, you'll be tempted for an instant. After all, what have you got to lose? Of course, the optimystic knows that if you succumb to the threat of the chain letter, you've lost far more than a few bucks in postage and copying and an hour of your time. You've lost your sense of inner poise and personal power, not to mention your common sense. By becoming a link in the chain, you've chained yourself to a destructive belief in the power of superstition to determine your destiny.

You'd think you'd have to be born yesterday to go for this hooey, but the sad fact of the matter is that armies of people are forever sending out those letters or spending hard-earned money to hear somebody tell them that their lucky day is right up ahead. Chain letters can be used for something positive, such as sending money out to charities, yet the spirit in which it is done has to be looked at. We would all be much luckier if we understood that, like Dorothy, who had to travel all the way to a bogus wizard to discover that only she could make her own dreams come true, there is no Oz. When it comes to luck, we need to be told and told and told again: We alone are the creators or destroyers of our luck; we alone are responsible for our own happiness or suffering. No horoscope can determine our future; no psychic can bring us the peace and security that we crave and that we continually search for in the dangerous realms of external gratification. True luck is an internal phenomenon, based on our chosen actions and attitudes. When we grow in wisdom, we grow in luck. When we know when to put forth effort and when to let go, when to move forward and when to retreat, how to make the most of whatever stage of the process that we are in, then we are the luckiest people of all, for we have learned the art of spiritual warriorship, the art of respectfully integrating our human talents with the divine timetable.

Winning the Lottery

Do you suffer from the lottery mentality? The lottery mentality is a form of magical thinking that is an extension of the victim mentality. While it is not motivated by superstition to the degree of the chain letter mentality, it is motivated by a fear of scarcity as well as the same misguided belief in luck being the result of a random occurrence. When we play the lottery, what we are essentially saying is, (a) I don't have control over my destiny, the lottery does; and (b) when I win the lottery, my troubles will be over. My life will be perfect.

If you play the lottery, you might stop to ask yourself why you believe that money and luck are synonymous and that prosperity is always good. Of course, this notion is so ingrained in our psyches that no matter how much we renounce in our spiritual life, there will be a remnant of this thinking left. And there are certainly bonuses to having money. You get better health care, and better food to eat, so you may feel better. More money may mean more time to enjoy yourself, allowing you access to the finer things in life. Optimystics are not averse to having money. But they know that it will not solve all their problems and that it may even create more unless they are spiritually centered. When we have all the money we think we want, we often find ourselves bored and restless, bereft of the exciting challenge that acquiring the money brought into our life. We realize that the real fun was in the hunt, not in the capture. So we have to set new goals, create new worlds to conquer. This is the critical juncture, the fork in the road where the adults are separated from the children, spiritually speaking. When you're finally rolling in dough, four paths lie before you. You can take the William Randolph Hearst route outlined in *Citizen Kane,* buying up the whole world and putting it in storage. You can be satisfied with what you have. You can become a philanthropist, giving to worthy causes or going out to do active service now that you never have to work again. Or you can decide that since you've been there and done that, it's finally time to chuck it all and check in to your own little cell in the abbey, to spend your final days in search of the inner contentment that material wealth never did provide after all.

And remember, while you're busy winning the lottery, somebody else isn't winning. The lottery is definitely not in the category of win-win negotiating; someone's good fortune is always made at the expense of the many. It might seem a dream come true to get that phone call from God, informing you that you've got thirty million dollars coming to you over the next twenty years. But have you ever stopped to think of what really goes into your having big money? We may think that it is fine to have tons of money and live it up now, but if any of that money came to us by way of harm to others, we may be in big trouble someday, even if we aren't consciously aware that others had to suffer for our good time. Hoarding is also something repellent to God, who reminds us time and again of the perils of storing treasures on earth; as Jesus said, "For where your treasure is, there will your heart be also" (Matthew 6:21).

The optimystic takes all the realms of existence into consideration, knowing that the life we are leading now will affect what we have on the other side and paying close attention to karma. This means that we have some work to do, because so many important things to consider are often not obvious to us. As optimystics, we understand that because we are part of the whole, and the whole is a part of us, what is given to one is given to all. We understand that money is designed to circulate; while we may make it and enjoy it, we will not allow it to rule our hearts.

Affirmative Action

For decades, we've heard about the power of positive affirmations. The idea is that if you affirm something long enough, it will happen and you will attract prosperous situations to you by the way you think. It's great to follow positive affirmations, stating what you want to create in life, but if you're a true optimystic, you know you also have to take a little affirmative action if you want those affirmations to come true. And often what is required from us in order to make these affirmations come true are actual changes in our behavior.

Most of the time these changes do not involve huge leaps in consciousness. More often than not, the issues that catch us up are usually very simple. Some people have trouble returning phone calls; others can't bring themselves to manage money and pay bills;

others can't say no when they have to. These may seem like minor personality flaws, but when we want to create large-scale success and happiness for ourselves, we have to address the little things that have the nasty habit of getting underfoot and tripping us up. The process of honest self-examination is crucial to the process of transforming our affirmations into reality. We can't really move forward until we face our fears. As optimystics, we know that in order to make full use of our immense capacity for change, we must make the effort to see ourselves from the vantage point of reality, not wishful thinking or denial. We know that we aren't perfect, that nobody is, and that therefore we don't have to run away in terror or shame from the dark corners of our psyche. All we have to do is turn on the lights—and then get out the dynamite!

Securing Our Place in the Eternal Future

The optimystic is fully cognizant of the fact that when it comes to eternal life, the future is now. If our mystic selves know that we are not our bodies, that we are indeed immortal in the soul sense of the word, our optimystic selves greet this life as a great way to prepare for the next one. After all, the only plausible explanation for being on this planet is that it's a great big school where we get the invaluable chance to learn our lessons in spiritual deportment. Then, if we pass our exams, we move up accordingly, in the direction of higher consciousness. So it definitely behooves us to become more and more aware of our present thoughts and actions.

The psychic hot lines will be quick to assure you that you'll have loads of material riches. But which of those psychics would have the nerve to say, "I see inner peace coming your way. . . . I see you doing good all over the planet. . . . Heck, you don't have a whole lot of money—in fact, you'll be one step ahead of the creditors your whole life, sorry—but that doesn't matter because you'll be accumulating so much spiritual wealth that, honey, let me tell you, when it's your time to go, you'll be able to buy the biggest spa in heaven!"

The fact remains, though, that when we do leave our physical form, we'll be traveling extra light. As the song has it, "there ain't no luggage racks on a hearse; there ain't no pockets on a shroud." We can't take *it* with us, but we certainly do take our scorecard. We'll be applauded not for how much money we made, but for how much money we shared; the points we get will be for how sincerely and selflessly we loved, not how self-important we became. So if we want to be really lucky, in terms of our eternal reward, all we have to do is start living in genuine optimystic fashion, right here, right now. Because optimystics know that the luckiest among us is the one who loves and is loved, from the depths of the human heart, they are not afraid to open their hearts to the widest F-stop, to take in the full panorama of joy and pain that are part and parcel of earthly life, and, in the process, to let in all the light they can.

Above all, the real optimystic triumph is to be able to work within the bounds of human frailty. Being of the Earth, we will always experience cycles of happiness and unhappiness, periods of feast and famine. There is no question that at times in our lives we feel like the gods are smiling down on us. Things may go well for no reason. It may be that we have fallen in love and we feel like we are invincible or that we feel extraordinarily lucky to be given the chance to work at what we love. Correspondingly, there are those times in which nothing seems to go right and the gods might be mocking us, when we feel despair because we are still attached to things outside ourselves and outside our relationship with the Creator. It may not be possible to fully transcend these cycles; no matter how advanced we become, how many hours of meditation we do, we can't escape the fact that the human experience is one of attachment. Yet our ultimate power comes in realizing this and learning how to adjust the level of our attachment. So flexibility is important to the optimystic; since life is change, the more flexible we can be in body, mind, and spirit, the more open we can be to the blessings that come our way, in all shapes, sizes, and disguises.

14

Spiritual Litter Is Against the (Natural) Law

If you think there is a solution you are part of the problem.

GEORGE CARLIN

Spiritual litterers are people who think they and they alone have all the answers to everyone's spiritual questions and dilemmas. They are the ones who scatter their tracts in the streets trying to share their solutions with everyone. Since humans, in general, try to avoid discomfort, many like the idea of a solution to their problems. After all, who wants to remain in doubt, in limbo, or just plain frustrated? Bring on the solution—any solution!

The only trouble is, this reliance upon solutions or fixes too often leads to addictive behaviors and dependency on what we perceive of as the answer to our difficulties. And spiritual solutions are no different. When Karl Marx called religion "the opiate of the people," he had a specific reason for equating religion with a severely addicting drug that anesthetized its users to life. Marx saw religion as the enemy of growth and awakening. In demanding obedience to its stifling rules and regulations and in making priests and other high officials the ones with the power, religion became a form of autocracy and tyranny, stripping the people of their own natural rights, their own power to think, reason, grow, and expand. It made them passive participants in life rather than active agents for change.

Relying on our spiritual beliefs as a form of rescue or fix makes us unable to accept the validity of others' beliefs or growth processes. At the same time, it may blind us to our own need for self-exploration and a deeper understanding of our own natures. The reward for this type of spiritual smugness is not paradise but rather a terminal case of tunnel vision.

For this reason, optimystics are not in the habit of going door-to-door with spiritual solutions. We don't litter the streets with tracts; we are not out to cut a new notch on our belts for each mind we convert to our way of thinking. We do not have the road map to everyone else's spiritual journey. We respect spiritual emergencies as the domain of providence. We simply behave according to the highest good in each interaction with others, allowing God to do the rest. For God works in mysterious ways, and humans work in circles unless they help God work.

Why Does Spiritual Littering Hurt Us So Much?

Why is it so frustrating to meet someone with an opposing spiritual view? You'd think that you'd both be on the same side, because you both want the spiritual best. Yet some of the worst conflicts, not to mention actual wars, come from disagreements in spiritual belief. When people hold on to spiritual beliefs, to the point where they are locked into them, their lives freeze in time. When we believe that life must be a certain way or else, all our energy may go into trying to squeeze experiences into belief systems too narrow to accommodate them. So we end up spending all of our valuable time and energy trying to fit a square block into a round hole. What is left?

One cause of imbalance in belief systems is the tendency to go after the devil in others instead of developing the God in ourselves. It can be immensely gratifying to the ego to take on the work of converting or saving another person. It can also be conveniently self-distracting. It's really much harder work to save ourselves from our own illusions. That stone becomes awfully heavy in our hands when we're holding onto it instead of casting it. But that stone is really our own inflexibility, our own inability to grasp the true immensity of God, who defies categorization and refuses to be crammed into the tiny spaces of dogma.

How does spiritual littering hurt us? Usually by emphasizing what is negative instead of what is optimystic. For instance, it is humorous in a sad way that we can find the most information on the devil through religious crusaders who, in their zealous efforts to vanquish him, are really only giving him a lot of free publicity. And if, as we are told, there's no such thing as bad publicity, the devil comes out a winner—as he usually does when humans try to catch him. It's no coincidence that the devil is invariably portrayed as crafty and too clever for words; he snares his prey not by force but by cunning. And being human, we fall right into the trap, time and again.

Spiritual littering invariably involves pitting one belief system against another so that somebody has to come out a loser. Unfortunately, many people feel personally threatened when their religious belief system is challenged. Dogma, after all, is meant to be accepted without question and anxiously protected from the pollution of other possible views.

The optimystic sees the absurdity in all this. When religion is used as a threat, it has turned on itself. When someone else has to lose so that we can win in the spiritual arena, how do you think God is reacting? You'd better believe he or she is reaching for the spiritual Alka-Seltzer! Conversely, when we focus more on our own inner work and our own struggle to understand the universe, we cease projecting our fear out onto others. We become more peaceful and are better messengers of light and love. Secure in our own spirituality, we don't need to be threatened by other religions or beliefs.

Take a moment now to reflect upon what function your present spiritual belief system is performing in your life. Is it giving you strength or making you feel subtly victimized? Does it give you joy—vitality, meaning, a sense of higher purpose, a sense of peace? Or does it make you feel guilty because you're not good enough or are too far down on the enlightenment ladder or are always sinning and therefore displeasing God? Does your spiritual belief system give you enough to think about and work on with yourself without worrying about the salvation of other people? Or do you feel your mission is to convert others to your way of thinking?

Warning Signs of Spiritual Litter

★ *My way or else.* If you read something that says it is *the only true way* to lose weight or change your life, and it is attacking other systems, warning! Spiritual litter up ahead!

★ *Rushing Judgment Day.* So many people out there just can't wait for Judgment Day! They're so excited by the thought that one of these days everybody is going to "get theirs" that they end up making Judgment Day come early by judging others right here and now. Warning: When judgment raises its self-satisfied head, a big trash can of spiritual litter is about to be dumped on yours.

★ *Gossip.* Gossip is another dangerous form of judgmentalism; it makes the gossip feel superior to the one gossiped about. In essence, the gossip plays God without being the least bit like God, who has far more pressing concerns, like loving us the way we are. But if God did gossip about you, what do you think God would be saying? Imagine God talking about you to someone else; it's a good way to get an honest personal evaluation of where you are and where you'd like to be. And remember: when you listen to a gossip, or when you gossip yourself, you can be sure that *you* will be the next subject on somebody's gossip list.

★ *Strict adherence to rules and regulations.* Do you really believe that something as big as God needs to play by the rule book? Of course there are rules of right conduct that can't be broken without causing harm to someone or something. But the rules of spiritual litterers are designed not to teach you to live correctly, but to live according to their dogma. Optimystics know that sometimes rules are meant to be broken, to create a larger opening through which the spirit can enter our lives. Remember, to be spiritual means to be spirit-full—full of spirit, full of life. Warning: When rules and regulations kill rather than nurture life, get out your spiritual litter picker-upper.

★ *Black-and-white thinking.* Thinking in either-or terms goes along with strict adherence to rules and regulations and demanding "my way or else." Watch out for either-or scenarios, for blanket characterizations of good and evil. Spiritual litterers do not make room for complex reasoning, for shades of meaning, for new and bold thinking in either their lives or yours. Imagination is the enemy of the spiritual litterer, for in the imagination all things are possible, and in the world of the spiritual litterers, all things are possible only for those who believe—in their way of seeing things!

As Timothy Leary said, "Be very careful about locating good or God, right or wrong, legal or illegal, at your favorite level of consciousness." With that in mind, have some fun with the following list, and laugh at yourself if any of it sounds "oh-too-familiar."

Ten Stupid Ways to Pollute the Spiritual Environment

1. *Talk about fearful, tragic things relentlessly.* Doomsayers are big polluters of the spiritual atmosphere. If you find yourself in a doomsday mood, simply admit that you have a fear of death, promise yourself you will not let it rule you, and resolve to look for life's more positive attributes when you're ready.

2. *Report awful statistics to those who are in particular need of hope.* Instead of believing in the power of the spirit and the power of our own thought processes to transform situations, the spiritual litterer grips the spirit in the vise of statistics, squeezing the life out of it by denying it hope and encouragement. Stop obsessing about the news and its attending statistical reports. Instead, begin to see statistics as illusory phenomena, which we can change at will. Remember that encouragement is one of the great gifts we were given to help each one rise to his or her greatest good. The optimystic knows that God does not discourage, and therefore neither should you.

3. *Bore others with an insatiable need for attention.* When you feel like you need attention, realize that the only things we really *need* are: air, water, food, and shelter. Those who are constantly looking for attention invariably end up being their only source of attention. Spiritual warriors are good listeners; spiritual litterers listen only to themselves. Think

about how depleted you feel when you're around someone who is an attention hog. Such people drain your vital energy; they're spiritual vampires. Resolve to do the opposite when you are with others—to give rather than take away energy.

4. *Create envy or jealousy in others.* When you know someone is struggling with her or his career and yours happens to be going swimmingly, have some compassion and sensitivity. Refrain from rubbing it in; know that there is a time and place to discuss your good fortune and that it probably isn't now. Instead, empathize with your friend; we all experience cycles, and one day the tables may be turned. How would you want someone else to respond to you if your life wasn't in the best of places?

5. *Pity yourself in front of others.* Do you really want to be pitiful, which means pathetic, inferior, and insignificant? If so, what a pity! This is another negative form of attention getting that spiritual litterers indulge in. But spiritual warriors get attention from other, more positive sources, like spreading hope and enthusiasm and being genuinely concerned for others. Pity parties have notoriously poor attendance; usually only one guest shows up, and you can figure out who!

6. *Refuse to find humor in anything.* Is there anything sadder than a humorless human? Humor is one of the saving graces of humankind, right up there alongside faith, hope, and courage. Without humor there's really no life. Spiritual litterers tend to regard humor with the same suspicion they reserve for imagination. Humor is dangerous! It might trivialize God, who must be treated at all times with the utmost sobriety. But the optimystic knows that God must have the greatest sense of humor of all to have created this wild ride of a universe. Spiritual warriors see the humor in life and become lighter and freer because of it. Lighten your load, and someone else's, with a good dose of humor.

7. *Ignore inspiration.* As we have seen, *to inspire* means literally "to breathe life into" someone. Some spiritual litterers come under the guise of inspirational leaders, so watch for what they're inspiring in you. If it's faith in yourself and support of your own spiritual journey, great. But if inspirational speakers inspire only the fear of God in you or the false hope that by accepting their belief system you are guaranteed the quick fix of instant salvation, it's time to explore the difference between inspiration and indoctrination. As for yourself, how do you inspire or breathe life into others? Optimystics know that the best inspiration is a

living example; their goal is not to teach but to inspire through the daily conduct of their own lives.

8. *Steal a dream.* In aboriginal society, dream stealing is punishable by banishment from the tribe, a fate worse than death. But stealing dreams is a common occurrence in our society. The spiritual litterer routinely steals dreams, replacing them with rules and regulations, black-and-white thinking, and other roadblocks designed to impede our personal spiritual journeys and vision quests. But the spiritual warrior believes in dreams and enjoys seeing them become reality, knowing that every dream that is supported and realized opens the door further to another coming true.

9. *Try to rescue others from their pain.* Most of us don't like to see other people in pain. But pain often fuels growth. If we try to rescue others from their pain, however well intentioned our efforts, we may be doing them a disservice. Of course, somebody wallowing in pain can be a pain; often we want to take that person's pain away just to make it easier on ourselves. But more often than not, what the person in pain is saying is, Be here with me. Listen to me. Don't give me advice; just give me love. So next time, try to change the chemistry of the moment by simply being silent as a friend discusses a painful situation or nodding in quiet empathy. See if this doesn't help your friend find his or her own way out of the pain. By the same token, never diminish someone else's pain by saying how great that person has it compared to someone else, particularly you. Spiritual litterers can often be martyrs, convinced that their suffering is second to none. Spiritual warriors appreciate whatever distress someone else is going through as valid, and they do not judge it according to a pain scale.

10. *Act anxious and focus on time when you are with someone.* If you don't have the time to be with someone, then don't be with them. But if you are with them, then make the time to be with them, fully and completely. We often think we don't have the time for simple interactions with our fellow humans, but the fact is that it usually takes more time and energy trying to avoid interactions with others than it does enjoying their presence, which might be a gift that we weren't expecting. Anxiousness and clock watching are not part of the optimystic's repertoire of social graces. When you find yourself tuning out other people, tune in to yourself, your center. Draw that deep breath, calm down, and realize that anxiousness and time obsession are completely unnecessary in the realm of the spirit.

Are You Afraid of the Dark?

Some religious belief systems teach that the closer we come to the light, the more upset and harassing the forces of darkness become and the more we can expect their unwelcome visits. As a result, many people believe in a literal Satan who is always there hiding around the corner, with one foot out to trip them up just when they think they're entitled to happiness, success, or a meaningful, joyful life. This belief system is otherwise known as guilt, and the more guilt we feel, the more victimized we become. But the truth is that the only power this enemy has is what we give it. When we give the dark forces too much credit, they have too much spending power in our lives. It takes some inner work to root out the real devils—our own fears and insecurities about our right to happiness and success—but the optimystic knows it can and must be done and the only thing we really have to fear is our own ridiculousness.

Other people think that God is putting them through trials, that God has hand-picked a few humans to torment and that they happen to be one of the chosen. Of course, this is something we will never really know. But one fact remains pertinent: we are the ones causing most of our suffering through our attachment to our wants and to certain outcomes, especially rewards for good actions. Martyrdom is the extreme form of victimhood; martyrs believe that they are meant to suffer, that there is absolutely nothing they can do about it, and that there is something heroic in never being happy. They hold Christ up as the example of the ultimate martyr, who died for everyone else's sins. But the multidimensionality of Christ—the many facets of his personality, his vision, his mission—escape them entirely. The fact is that Jesus knew how to laugh, how to enjoy life and people, and that he definitely wanted us to understand the importance of celebrating life. True martyrdom—dying for a cause—may have its place, but wannabe martyrs, that is, whiners, are spiritual litterers, not spiritual warriors.

Another way of becoming stuck in the dark is constantly replaying a worn-out episode in our lives. The past can carry heavy weight that drags us and others down. Think about it: don't you think your friends are tired of hearing about all that past pain and suffering you went through at the careless hands of an old lover? Convincing yourself that the person was a jerk does not take away the pain of losing love, which is really what you are mourning. Many times we hang on to pain because it is the only reality left of the experience we so long to recapture in its better moments. Or we mistakenly believe that as long as we suffer, we won't forget. But the optimystic deals with what is really lost so that he or she can heal and move on. If there is a situation in your life that you can't seem to get over, try looking at the real issues involved. If you're holding a grudge, ask yourself what payoff you're getting from your anger and what bigger payoff you might get from letting it go. Remember that your attitude toward a situation is your choice. There is no reward in hanging on to past misery; pain is useful only as a lesson, not as an albatross.

Mean People Are Human Litter

"Mean people suck" is a saying we find from time to time on bumper stickers or T-shirts. Meanness does indeed spread a tremendous amount of negative litter. What exactly is meanness? And, correspondingly, what is niceness?

In the dictionary we find one definition of the word *mean* to be "lacking in elevating human qualities, as kindness and goodwill." We all know that life is hard; taking it out on one another makes it worse. So the choice is ours. We can be mean, or we can be honest, awake, and compassionate.

On the other hand, are you suffering from "nice pollution"? Have you, like we, gotten sick of the word *nice?* Nice is how we describe someone who does what we want them to do, someone who does not cause us agitation or disagree with us. Often niceness is not honest because it creates dependency and attachment. When we choose something based on how nice it is for us, we may be allowing ourselves to be victims or helpless infants. Similarly, if we're always trying to be nice, we may be secretly manipulating others, controlling them through guilt and obligation. If you want others to think of you as a nice person, or if you expect others to always be nice to you, you might want to explore niceness a bit. It's fine to be courteous and compassionate. But if niceness becomes a fogging mechanism for honesty, it's time to reexamine your expectations of how you and others "should" behave.

Optimystics not only pick up and throw out spiritual litter; they leave something beautiful behind in its place. This is where kindness becomes the best-known antidote to spiritual littering. Doing "random acts of kindness" is catching on in our society, and we hope the trend continues. One little act of kindness can go on sending healing energy for miles. How wonderful it is to surprise our fellow humans with beauty, love, and graciousness!

Creating Your Spiritual Legacy

We are always in the process of creating our spiritual legacy. Our words and actions live beyond us in the lives and memories of others, many of whom we have never met and will never meet. At every moment, we are building our spiritual legacy, affecting others who live beyond us in ways we may not ever know.

1. What would your spiritual legacy be if you left the physical realm right now? A good way to assess this is to imagine the stories others might tell of you at this very moment. What acts of kindness did you perform that people might remember or that you'd like them to remember? Write them down. What acts might be remembered that you'd rather were forgotten? Write them down too.

2. How can you begin today to create the spiritual legacy you really want to leave behind you? Make a chart with two columns, one marked "Keep," the other "Change." What are the best things about you that you can think of? What habits or attitudes could stand an overhaul? Make the appropriate entries in each column.

3. Reflect upon the following questions: Do I think I am important in the grand scheme of things? Do I take the time to consider the effect,

immediate and long range, that my actions and words will have on others? Do I really believe in the interconnectedness of all things? Sit with these questions awhile; they are important, for they form the basis of your spiritual legacy. If you can't answer yes to all of them, ask yourself, What in these questions is difficult for me to believe or accept? Why?

4. Begin a daily legacy ledger, in which you enter all acts of kindness, random and otherwise, that you have given the world. Don't use this ledger to dwell on the things you didn't or should have done; rather, accentuate the positive until it becomes a natural part of your daily routine. Your ledger might have entries like, "Complimented my waitress and told her how good she is at her work"; "Bought an unexpected gift for a co-worker"; "Asked the elderly lady across the street if she needed anything from the store"; "Gave some money to the rescue mission"; and so on. At the end of a week, go over the ledger and reflect upon the good that you do without even thinking about it as well as the positive changes you have made in the universe and in yourself in just seven days. Imagine the effect you will have on the world for the rest of your life. Good luck!

O 15

Self-Serve or Full Service?

*Enlightenment—the perfection of wisdom, the direct under-
standing of the true nature of reality, and compassion, the open
feeling of connection with other beings that results from such direct understanding. This wisdom creates the enlightened mind,
which is omnipresent, blissful, omniscient, and technically in-
conceivable to any human mentality.*

ROBERT A. F. THURMAN

Many of us think of service and compassion in terms of volunteer
work, which of course we don't have time for, so we dismiss the
idea altogether. Or we perceive of service as a grand global gesture,
like Mother Teresa taking on Calcutta or Clara Barton devoting her
life to the Red Cross. But the optimystic knows that opportunities
for spiritual service are always present when we go out among others. We don't need to travel far; in fact, if everyone practiced true
compassion just with their friends and the people in their neighborhood, this world would be in infinitely better shape.

Spiritual service starts simply. A smile we beam at someone
may change that person's day and save her or him from despair.
Letting someone know you care is like a magic balm for the soul.
It is a source of great satisfaction to be part of the force that keeps
love moving in the world. Take a moment to look at the part

service plays in your life now. What were today's kindnesses given and received?

In a world where selfless devotion to others is too often the exception rather than the rule, it is essential to cultivate the transcendent properties of compassion. Most of the problems in this world stem from an inability to empathize with others' pain. Until we are willing to open ourselves to the suffering of others and take action to alleviate it, we cannot be truly spiritual and the world's misery cannot be healed. But compassion does not, unfortunately, come easily to human beings. Why not, we don't know; you'd think God would have made it a high priority in all of us. But instead compassion seems to be a learned behavior, absorbed through role models and teachings that open the heart to the true nature of love.

Divine Love

The world as a whole has forgotten the real meaning of the word love. . . . You have not understood how to develop love, how to purify and expand it into divine love.

Paramahansa Yogananda, The Divine Romance

Divine love flows out of the mystic union with God. When we experience this union, it is as if we have stepped out of the fog of ego into the sunlight of unconditional love. Because we have known the ultimate in love, we are able to see the world through love's eyes. As Yogananda says, when you really know God's love on the level not of the intellect but of the soul, "You will commune with all nature, and you will love equally all mankind . . . your brothers and sisters in Him."

But if we have not witnessed or experienced compassion in our lives, how can we be compassionate? Most people can't; we see the bitter fruits of selfishness and hatred all around us. From the neighborhoods of Jerusalem and Sarajevo and the villages of Rwanda to the streets of our own cities, human life is cheap because anger and fear have overtaken reason. This is why optimysticism is so crucial today, as an urgent reminder of the value of all human beings as children of God and of our ensuing obligation to practice love and compassion at every level of our lives.

The Mystic Power of Compassion

The origin of the word *compassion* is the Latin *compati,* meaning "to sympathize or empathize with." Compassion is an awakening of the heart that moves one from untamed self-interest toward a sense of shared humanity. Compassion is the will to free others from their suffering, based on an empathetic sensitivity to that suffering. Its opposites are hatred, which is wanting others to suffer, and indifference, not caring about the welfare of others. The truly compassionate person feels another's pain. When we experience the unity of self and other, the suffering of others becomes our own, and compassion becomes a natural response.

Compassion is important not just because it is necessary to care about others; compassion is the fundamental *spiritual* experience.

> Compassion is no attribute. It is the LAW of Laws—eternal Harmony, a shoreless, universal essence, the light of everlasting Right, and fitness of all things, the law of love eternal. Compassion is a tender solicitude, a dedicated resolve to return good for evil and to add nothing to the unhappiness of any living creature.
> (Manly P. Hall, *Buddhism and Psychotherapy*)

Compassion is the lesson we are all here to learn. It is the most practical way to bring the reality of mystic transcendence of the self into daily living, because it echoes the transcendental experience, taking us out of ourselves and uniting us with others. In the process, we benefit from the compassion we feel. We attract love and compassion into our own lives; the old phrase "what you give is what you get" couldn't be more applicable here, as the more loving-kindness we generate, the more comes back to us. And the more compassionate we become, the more deeply and richly we understand our higher purpose, which is, first and foremost, to love.

The Bodhisattva Path

A bodhisattva, or "servant of peace," is a living archetype of compassion. The Sanskrit word comes from *bodhi,* meaning "enlightenment," which is the combination of wisdom and compassion, and *sattva,* "a hero or heroine." Out of compassion, a bodhisattva resolves not to abandon the world of form after attaining enlightenment but to retain a physical or energetic body for assisting fellow beings on the spiritual path. The bodhisattva's unselfish service yields continuous karmic merit, which is replenished with every act of compassion and is thus inexhaustible.

A Bodhisattva with a capital *B* refers to a bodhisattva such as the East Asian goddess Kuan Yin, who has nearly or actually become a Buddha. These are angelic deities who reach out to us or provide us with role models for reaching out to others as we become enlightened. But, as John Blofield, scholar and author of *Bodhisattva of Compassion: The Mystical Tradition of Kuan Yin,* observes, Kuan Yin is "far from being a figure of poetic whimsy. Yogically she corresponds to an actual energy permanently latent in the mind. . . . The sheer beauty of the concept of an exquisitely lovely being whose chief attribute is pure, unwavering compassion is in itself appealing enough to claim our admiration."

The name *Kuan Yin,* which means "she who hearkens to the cries of the world," comes from *Kuan,* the Chinese word for earth, and *Yin,* the unswerving feminine power that balances the masculine Yang energy. It is said that the loving-kindness emanating from the Bodhisattva Kuan Yin is so powerful that the mere repetition of her name will bring the qualities of her mercy, generosity, and peace into one's life, along with the banishment of fear and hardship. Kuan Yin reminds us that we are unconditionally loved and nurtured by the Divine Mother regardless of what we do. So don't be afraid to call on this unbounded source of love and compassion whenever you need it.

While in Buddhist tradition the bodhisattva has traditionally been considered a higher being, humans are nonetheless encouraged to work at attaining bodhisattva-hood. The ancient Tibetan Buddhist texts outline an arduous training program for bodhisattvas-in-the-making, with strict teachings for behavior along the path. "The Thirty-seven-fold Practice of a Bodhisattva" is a difficult ascetic undertaking of intense inner work that involves daily meditation and solitude and relinquishing the concerns of this life. But the goal of the bodhisattva is not isolation but liberation. Like all great spiritual teachers, bodhisattvas temporarily retreat from the world in order to free themselves of grasping desires that would otherwise keep them chained to their egos and their false sense of self. When bodhisattvas discover their true self, all sense of separateness ceases and they reemerge into the world with the one all-consuming desire to take on the suffering of others—even that of their enemies.

> If someone driven by great desire
> Seizes all my wealth . . .
> To dedicate to him my body, possessions
> And past, present and future merit is the practice of a
> Bodhisattva.
> Even if someone cuts off my head
> When I am not the least at fault
> To take all his negative actions
> Compassionately upon myself is the practice of a
> Bodhisattva.
>
> *From "The Thirty-seven-fold Practice of a Bodhisattva,"*
> *translated by Gyelse Togme*

This is perhaps the most remarkable message of the bodhisattva—that we should not only pray for our enemies but also take on their negative karma and suffering. While it may seem like the extreme opposite of assertiveness training, and while most of us, when faced with an aggressor, might prefer to look out for our own welfare and the welfare of those we love, the lesson of the bodhisattva is nonetheless a compelling one. It is only through complete and selfless compassion that we can genuinely become one with all beings, to the point where we cease judging anyone or anything. And it is at the critical point when we are free of judgment that we become free to truly serve.

The Girl Scout as Bodhisattva

In *The Tibetan Book of Living and Dying*, Sogyal Rinpoche says,

> What the world needs more than anything is bodhisattvas, active servants of peace . . . dedicated to their bodhisattva vision and to the spreading of wisdom in all reaches of our experience. We need bodhisattva lawyers, bodhisattva artists and politicians . . . doctors and economists . . . teachers and scientists . . . technicians and engineers, working consciously as channels of compassion and wisdom at every level and in every situation of society . . . working for the preservation of our world and for a more merciful future.

His Holiness the Dalai Lama expands upon the idea and importance of the bodhisattva in today's world:

> The various features and aspects of human life, such as longevity, good health, success, happiness, and so forth, which we consider desirable, are all dependent on kindness and a good heart. These are basic qualities of human nature. It is also very clear that for a bodhisattva to be successful in accomplishing the practice of the six perfections—generosity, ethical discipline, tolerance, joyous effort, concentration, and wisdom—cooperation with and kindness towards sentient beings are extremely important.

What better example of a bodhisattva could be found than the Girl Scout, whose famous pledge embodies all of these ideals?

The Girl Scout Pledge

On my honor, I will try:
To do my duty to God and my country,
To help other people at all times,
To obey the Girl Scout Laws.

The Girl Scout laws involve important bodhisattva attributes like integrity ("A Girl Scout's honor is to be trusted"), loyalty ("She can be entrusted with a confidence"), friendship ("A Girl Scout is a friend to all and a sister to every other Girl Scout"), respect ("A Girl Scout is courteous; she shows consideration for others although their ideas, beliefs, and ways of living are different from hers"). Above all, the Girl Scout is a servant of compassion. It is no less than her "duty" to "be useful and to help others."

Although it might not have been consciously intended as such, the *Girl Scout Handbook* is a bodhisattva guide to living. (By the way, being girls, we didn't have the *Boy Scout Handbook* on hand, but it follows the same principles.) It constantly reminds its young readers that they are part of a larger plan, a bigger world, and that they have an obligation to make that world a better place—a place of integrity and spiritual consciousness-raising, a place that is safe for others, a place where compassion and understanding are the basic values of existence. The pledge, which runs the risk of sounding corny, is explained in the handbook in a way that leaves no doubt: once upon a time, our society knew the principles of the bodhisattva and knew that instilling them in young people was crucial to the merciful future of the planet.

On my honor: It is easy to make a promise. To keep a promise may be difficult unless you understand it. When you are invested as a Girl Scout and make this Promise, you are saying . . . I can be trusted to do and mean what I say, even though it may not always be easy.

To do my duty to God: I will honor God in the finest way I know and will be faithful to my own religion.

. . . And my country: I will try to make my country a place where everyone can live and work in safety and freedom.

To help other people at all times: I will think of ways I can help others. I will think of others first and not myself.

To obey the Girl Scout Laws: I know that I have taken a code of honor. I will try to live by the code.

The Dalai Lama would have made a great scout leader. "The entire message of the buddhadharma," he explains in *The Path to Bliss,* "can be summed up in two succinct statements: 'Help others' and 'If you cannot help them, at least do not harm them.'" Of course, this is the basic premise of all religions. We exist not as individual entities but as a part of the whole; everything we do and say has consequences, effects on the world around us, from the present moment to future generations. We all thus have an obligation—a duty—to obey the Girl Scout laws—"generosity, ethical discipline, tolerance, joyous effort, concentration, and wisdom"—for they are nothing less than the spiritual laws of cooperation with and kindness toward sentient beings. So the principles of the bodhisattva—the principles of service to humankind—extend to all cultures. Why? Because they are the foundation for life on this planet. Without them there are no moral codes, no ethical standards, no models for truly loving behavior. Without them there is no basis for a satisfactory spiritual, let alone an earthly, life. Compassion truly is the foundation of a spiritual life, because without it we can never really understand the teachings of the great spiritual teachers, no matter how well read we are. Kindness is a living ideal established in spiritual law. Negative attitudes are wrong not merely because they cause unhappiness, but because they are contrary to the eternal pattern, the right feeling that is embodied in the bodhisattva virtues.

How can *you* become a bodhisattva? By beginning, like a good scout, to live these virtues to the best of your ability and to bring them into your work. You—yes, you—can be a bodhisattva teacher, a bodhisattva lawyer, a bodhisattva store clerk, bringing compassion to everyone you meet and "generosity, ethical discipline, tolerance, joyous effort, concentration, and wisdom" to everything that you do. All it takes is the earnest desire to be more loving and caring toward others. This desire will always lead you in the right direction.

Deep Understanding Unlocks the Heart

Thich Nhat Hanh points out,

> In the Bible, when someone touches Christ, he or she is healed. It is not just touching that brings about a miracle. When you touch deep understanding and love, you are healed.

Deep understanding brings us compassion, and this is the true beginning of healing and the connection of souls. Without compassion, you may come upon interesting techniques but not a deeper healing.

Compassion is alive in our hearts, available for action at all times. When we tap into our compassion, we carry a healing energy with us wherever we go. This energy is so powerful that we may never know how far it reaches into the souls of others and what transformations can occur because of it. For instance, children who had a horrendous childhood yet turned out to be loving and successful adults tell of at least one person in their childhood who showed them kindness and love, maybe only briefly, but whose sincere compassion made them believe in themselves.

We operate on so many levels, many of which are unconscious, that it is important to realize how powerful our intentions are.

Sometimes we send out prayers for others without realizing it, for often when we wish something for someone, we radiate unconscious energy in their direction. So one moment of good wishes for another, one moment of true caring for another, can affect that person in ways that we may never have expected. The same is true of malicious wishes. We are in charge of our spiritual energy. The more conscious we are of our intent, and the more conscious we are of having a pure heart, the better we make the world.

One of the emotions that keeps our heart locked and removed from deep understanding is anger. At its most basic, anger is simply energy. It is often associated with fire and heat, qualities also associated with the spirit. As such, it can be a source of creative, even spiritual expression. Anger is a feeling like any other feeling, and it carries with it the power to illuminate or destroy. It is a form of passion, and our best chemistry comes when passion is transformed into compassion.

Why does it seem so much easier at times to choose anger rather than love and forgiveness? First of all, it often just plain feels good to yell and scream or to feel righteous indignation. It "fires" us up, makes us feel alive. Anger can be a kind of fuel, spurring us on to action that we ordinarily would not have taken. It is indeed often easier to be angry than to be understanding or forgiving, because anger is like a drug, rewarding us with an adrenaline rush. Anger is also an instantaneous reaction; it takes time and effort to disengage ourselves from its seductive embrace. Forgiveness, on the other hand, is an acquired virtue, which comes with patience, insight, and the honest desire to move past anger and toward healing.

It is not wrong to feel angry; it's what we do with our anger and what we allow it to do to us that determines whether or not it will be a helpful or a harmful energy source. When we express our anger appropriately, we defuse its harmful potential, and we can turn it into a source of creative energy as well as a means of improving relationships and communication. But suppressed or misdirected anger is a breeding ground for physical, psychological, and spiritual unhappiness. Both unexpressed and unchecked anger may find a violent way out of the soul, taking the form of physical or mental abuse or making itself heard through illness, depression, or, in its most tragic outcry, suicide.

A pessimistic view of life can result from anger that has not been dealt with appropriately. But the optimystic accepts that sometimes this happens, since there's a pessimist somewhere inside all of us. Before we can be agents of compassion, we have to be able to accept all the feelings and emotions that go along with being human. And it definitely wouldn't be human to always be a bundle of cheer. So at those times when you're feeling pessimistic, why not let yourself rant and rave? Go ahead—complain your heart out! You can't look on the bright side with a boulder of anger obstructing your view.

When you really want to let your inner pessimist out, here's a good exercise. Find a friend who allows you the luxury of calling him or her just to rant and rave. Make this friend the manager of the Complaint Department. Make the following agreement between you: The next time you feel the urge to sink your teeth into the world's ankle, you will first ask the code question, "Is the complaint department open?" If your friend is in the mood to be your sounding board, the answer will be "Yes, go ahead." If your friend says, "I'm sorry, the department is closed at the moment, but I'll call you back when it's open," it's a message to respect your friend's boundaries and not take advantage of a willing ear.

Remember the optimystic chemistry lab? This little exercise can change the chemistry of pessimism faster than anything else, because it invariably leads to laughter as well as to a clue or two to the real reason behind your resentment or unhappiness. The important thing is that both parties know that this is a venting time and that the ultimate goal is to return to the real issue and make a change. In other words, don't play this game unless you really want your complaints to lead you to a more positive outlook. Frustration and anger can overwhelm us to the point where we become depressed and shut down. The more you practice handling anger in a positive way, the more life energy can flow through you and the more optimystic you will become.

Above all, remember that anger often accompanies compassion. When Mother Teresa saw the conditions of the sick and dying in India, she was angry—angry enough to become a lesson in compassion to the rest of the world. Anger is not the opposite of compassion; it can be the force that opens up the floodgates of compassion. The truly compassionate person respects anger for what it is and uses it for purposes of redemption, not destruction.

What Helps?

The best thing we can do for other human beings is simply to be present in the moment with them. One of the tough things about feeling compassion is that when we let ourselves feel the pain of others, we may become so full of pain ourselves that we immediately judge the situation negatively. We may want to rescue someone from pain rather than allowing them to be with and learn from their experience. Another's painful situation gives us the splendid opportunity to get into our "don't know mind" and admit that we don't know the real reason for suffering or the mysterious healings and revelations that might come about because of it. Our task as an optimystic is to listen empathetically and just let the other person know that we are there. This is often all that a suffering person really wants—someone who listens, someone who cares.

Bodhisattva training is rigorous because it takes a long time to learn the secret of taking on the suffering of others without falling apart ourselves. There are times when you are perfectly justified in feeling that you can't save the world and that it's time to pull back and gather your own resources. Yes, Jesus carried the sins of the world on his shoulders—but he was Jesus. Allow yourself to ask questions like, Is it feasible to go around with a heart broken open with unconditional compassion? Is this something to strive for? Can I handle that much angst and pain? Do I have the ability to feel deep compassion while still protecting my own health, both psychic and physical? Is compassion best on a grand scale, or is it the little seeds of kindness we sow each day that make the greatest difference?

If we're facing roadblocks along the route to a compassionate response to life, it may be because those obstacles are, for the moment, a necessary protective mechanism. We may want to respect such obstacles when they appear, listening to what they have to tell us rather than trying to circumvent them or bulldoze them out of our path. After all, we're all feeling our way through life. As opti-mystics, we can allow ourselves the luxury of pulling back from a particularly painful situation, trusting that when we are ready we may be able to move even deeper into the realm of compassion.

When in Doubt, Pray

Prayer is one of the most important mystical things we can do to encourage compassion. Ask yourself the following questions: Do you feel comfortable talking with God? Does praying seem compli-cated to you? Do you have to be part of a religion to pray? Can your life itself be a prayer? What does prayer mean to you?

Prayer allows us true communication with God. Praying on a consistent basis assures that we won't get too far away from the true source of life and love. Prayer keeps us grounded and on track. There is no one way to pray; there are prayers of forgiveness, grati-tude, understanding, help, direction, guidance, and surrender. Your prayer experience will suffer if you worry that you are praying the wrong way or that you don't know who you are praying to. Pray when you feel doubt, but do not doubt God. Do not try and second-guess God or answer your own prayers. We don't really need to know exactly how and why prayer works. Our souls just know, while our spirits guide us in the type of prayer that is best for our situa-tion. Our logical minds might be left confused, but give conscious-ness a little more credit.

Some people pray because they think they will get good results. They believe that God wants them to have everything they want, so all they have to do is ask. We believe it's actually the other way around. When we pray, we tune in to what God wants, and we declare that although we may not know exactly what that requires, we are willing to find out. This takes a lot of courage and the agreement to change, grow, and evolve. When we pray to God for something, we are praying for the highest spiritual good to take place. So the actual thing we want won't come to pass because it was not best for our spiritual growth or the growth of the person we were praying for.

One of the most effective ways to help, in a situation where we feel helpless, is to pray. If we hear of a family that needs so much help that we don't know where to start, a sincere prayer is a good thing to offer first. If we hear of great injustices and bloodshed in the world, we can ask in prayer that the perpetrators have a change of heart, a spiritual conversion. We often think that prayer isn't working if we don't see instant, visible results. But we need to keep in mind that humans have free will and that we cannot see how God is working in their hearts.

Prayer may seem elusive to you until you make it an integral part of your everyday life. When you become more aligned with your mystic self, you may experience prayer as a powerful force of light or a source of ecstasy and peace. The ultimate reason for praying is not to have our petitions granted but to open the channels of communication between ourselves and God. Ideally, prayer is not a one-sided conversation but a communication—a communion. Through prayer, we are not only speaking to God; God is speaking to us. When we really begin to hear and feel God in our lives and thoughts, we move to another level of prayer, one that is more contemplative, more *receiving* of God. In the process, we begin to respond with spontaneous compassion toward each and every one of our fellow creatures, who all are recipients of divine love.

Compassion thus becomes a way of serving both God and our fellow humans. To serve in a full and meaningful way does not mean that we are out combing the planet for people in dire need; it is equally if not more important to understand and care for those close by. Think of yourself as forever on call for God. Keep a part of you awake at all times to what your calling may require. You can even think of yourself as an angel in training, or a bodhisattva in the making, using your experience as a human in the best possible way—which will be a personal expression uniquely your own. Have fun with compassion, with God, and with the angels; help them and they will help you. Let your compassion reach out to the Earth and all the beauty of its fragile systems. Through prayer, feel at one with God; through compassion, feel at one with all of creation.

16

Let the Glad Games Begin

Just breathing isn't living.

POLLYANNA

On your optimystic travels, don't be surprised if someone, some-where, sometime accuses you of being a Pollyanna. Probably all of us are familiar with this derogatory term that is so often, and so mistakenly, used to dismiss the optimist as a naive idealist whose perception of reality is distorted by the rose-colored lenses of wish-ful thinking. But the more we thought about Pollyanna-ism, the more we realized that as a view of reality, it has its definite optimys-tic merits in presenting a hopeful view of the world and in proving that reality is not something that happens to us; it's something that we constantly create and change, through our beliefs and attitudes.

Pollyanna was a children's classic, written by Eleanor Hodgins Porter at the time of the First World War, about a cheery little girl who was the soul of optimism. A destitute orphan who was sent to live with her mean-spirited spinster aunt, Pollyanna managed to continually find hope and goodness in everything, no matter how dismal or insignificant. In fact, she had a curious, and not altogether unnauseating, way of turning "bad" things and people into "good" ones—of unearthing, like the world's most astute miner, the silver lining behind every cloud on the horizon of her lonely little life.

Pollyanna accomplished this admirable feat through a practice she referred to as the "glad game." This was a game her father had taught her before he died, and it consisted of finding something positive in every negative. For instance, when Pollyanna discovers that Aunt Polly doesn't approve of ice cream because she firmly believes that children shouldn't have too many treats, Pollyanna replies, "Oh well, I'm *glad* about that, because the ice cream you don't eat can give you an awful stomachache." When Aunt Polly punishes her for being late to dinner by banishing her to the kitchen for a meager meal of bread and milk, Pollyanna gets all excited because she likes bread and milk and is "glad" for the chance to eat it with Nancy, the kind hired girl. When Pollyanna gets a pair of crutches from the Ladies' Aid instead of the doll she requested, her glad reserves are temporarily threatened, but she rises to the occasion by being "glad I don't need 'em!" And on and on she goes, relishing the daily fresh challenges of the glad game and teaching it to everybody else, until the whole town eventually becomes one big hotbed of relentless gratitude.

For some strange reason, not only did *Pollyanna* become an instant sensation when it was first published in 1913, but the glad game took the world by storm. Glad Clubs sprang up everywhere. From the New York Stock Exchange to India, Pollyanna-ism became as infectious as the influenza epidemic that was sweeping the globe at the same time. In November 1918, Armistice month, *American Magazine* proclaimed Pollyanna's favorite pastime "the most popular game in the world." Somehow the brave little girl who kicked adversity in the butt with the steel boot of indefatigable optimism touched a mass nerve. She became a symbol of hope and courage in a world stunned by a war so terrible that people believed the likes of it would never be seen again.

But Pollyanna-ism had its limits. A Great Depression, a vast increase in organized and disorganized crime, and a Second World War were just some of the horrors waiting around the corner for a world that wanted desperately to believe that a round or two of the glad game would make it all go away. The question became, could

Pollyanna dare to play the glad game in the concentration camps? As society came apart at the seams and cynicism replaced idealism, Pollyanna and her glad game came to be associated with the most naive and dangerous aspects of positive thinking, until Pollyanna-ism and optimism were inexorably fused in the public consciousness.

But today, as we face the most cynical of worlds and the most perilous of times, might be a very good day to reexamine the message of *Pollyanna,* which was actually far more profound than is commonly realized. For Pollyanna reminds everybody what real living is all about. When Aunt Polly fills up Pollyanna's days with duties, Pollyanna protests in dismay,

> "Oh, but Aunt Polly, Aunt Polly, you haven't left me any time at all just to—to live."
>
> "To live, child! What do you mean? As if you weren't living all the time!"
>
> "Oh, of course I'd be breathing all the time I was doing those things, Aunt Polly, but I wouldn't be living. You breathe all the time you're asleep but you aren't living. I mean living—doing the things you want to do: playing outdoors, climbing hills, talking to Mr. Tom in the garden, and Nancy. . . . That's what I call living, Aunt Polly. Just breathing isn't living."

When you read between the lines of *Pollyanna,* you realize that, as is the case with most enduring children's classics, a powerful spiritual message is being delivered in the guise of a deceptively simple story. Much of the world *is* asleep, as any true mystic would tell you. Many people go through life sleepwalking—breathing but not waking up. If we have any duty at all as human beings, it is to enjoy life, to go beyond breathing into feeling, partaking of, and appreciating all of its wonders.

The truth, as we see it, is that Pollyanna was really the quintessential optimystic. In her determination to live as fully as possible, to find the best in everything and everyone, and to offer thanks and praise for the mystery of life, which to her was always a delightful surprise, Pollyanna became a miracle worker. She helped people who had lost all hope to find renewed purpose in life. She thawed out hearts frozen by years of repressed grief. She brought the light of love into the dark corners of locked-up souls. She taught everyone with whom she came in contact how to live with a passion and intensity that reconnected them to both Earth and heaven. In short, she raised the vibrations of the planet, uplifting not only an entire fictional town but also an entire real world that was so hungry for meaning that it devoured the Pollyanna message.

In a society paralyzed by fear of negative forces gone berserk, we seem to be acutely aware that the only way to reclaim control of our lives is to rekindle the flame of hope that is lit at the birth of every human soul and to spread its light and warmth around until, instead of perishing by fire, the world is enflamed with consciousness.

Pollyanna also reminds us that it's hard work to be an optimystic. It *isn't* always easy to play the glad game, especially when you're eleven and both your parents have died; there's more than one moment when her spirit falters and tears take over. But she invariably gives it over to God, surrendering to a higher meaning that she trusts will not always be beyond her grasp. Above all, Pollyanna is a *spiritual warrior.* She makes her way through the trenches of life with a resoluteness that inspires us to work through our pain and move beyond it, knowing that if we do, our reward will be healing and growth and a deeper appreciation for life's graces. Since we're here, we might as well *be here*, fully present, fully aware, fully receptive.

The glad game was initially tough for a lot of Pollyanna's grumpier acquaintances to take; it sounded so stupid. But like a Zen master's smack on the head, it led directly to enlightenment. The more people played it, the happier, more compassionate, and more grateful they became, not to mention more alive. And, like a Zen master, Pollyanna was continually practicing, living the game until it became a mantra in her heart, as natural as breathing. Therefore, as optimystics, we propose that it might be a good idea to resuscitate the glad game. Dig it up, dust it off, and revitalize it for a new millennium of players. After all, the only way you can lose is to not play at all.

How to Play the Glad Game

So how do you play the glad game? Well, Pollyanna's rules are as simple as only an eleven year old's—or a Zen master's—can be:

"The game is to just find something about everything to be glad about, no matter what 'tis."

Everything?

Yup. Everything. That's the best part of the game.

"The harder 'tis, the more fun 'tis!"

How long does it take to get the hang of it?

"Most generally it doesn't take so long . . . and lots of times now I just think of them without thinking, you know. I've got so used to playing it. It's a lovely game."

That's it in a nutshell. But we'd like to suggest a few revisions. First of all, as in any exercise you undertake, you should begin with a warm-up. In this case, the warm-up consists of an initial round of the "Not Glad Game," in which you allow yourself to have whatever feelings come up about the situation you've picked before you take the A-train to Happyland. For example, say your cat has just died. Instead of just rushing into a statement like, "I'm so *glad* my cat died because now I don't have to live with any more shredded furniture," let yourself feel whatever comes up. Sadness, anger, emptiness . . . get into the feeling. Start out with, "I'm not glad my cat died, be-cause I lost my most faithful companion." Don't suppress or deny these feelings; just be with them. Now, when you feel ready . . . On your mark, get set . . . Go! "I'm glad my cat died because . . ." Does it sound absurd? That's the whole point! A game like this has to be to-tally absurd in order to be meaningful. Go ahead. "I'm glad my cat died because I hated her throwing up on my clothes all the time! I'm glad my cat died because now I'll save a thousand bucks a year in vet bills! I'm glad my cat died because now my allergic boyfriend can fi-nally move in! I'm glad my cat died because I got a new kitten who gave me a new sense of life. I'm glad my cat died because the loss made me more aware of others' pain. I'm glad my cat died because she was so sick and now she's at peace."

The glad game actually goes beyond Pollyanna's childlike conception of it. The point is not to be glad for the actual misfortune—we must allow ourselves to mourn loss and adversity appropriately—but to appreciate the unexpected good things that might have come out of it. And if we can't think of any good things, we at least can appreciate the mystery that lies at the heart of the optimystic's experience of life. Forces you can't see or feel are still at work, explanations might not always be available or necessary, and you can still be glad for the opportunity to simply *surrender* to the unknowable, the place where, free of expectation and preconception, you may discover a new direction, a new purpose, a new self.

We are not suggesting that you be glad for horrible abominations or searing losses, only, eventually, for the chance to grow from these devastations. As the poet Rumi observed, your loss can be the garden of your compassion. Your tears can fertilize the soil of your soul. But only when you are ready. It may not be time yet to play the glad game over a particularly painful experience; the game is not intended as Band-Aid therapy.

The Glad Game as a Stress-Reduction Technique

A recent article in *Country Living's Healthy Living* profiled a stress-research center in Boulder Creek, Colorado, by the name of HeartMath. HeartMath views heart disease not as a dietary or physical disorder, but as an emotional phenomenon. According to the article,

> Research has shown that positive feelings can protect against heart disease and high blood pressure. Some studies have examined the heart's role beyond that of a muscle; they've explored its capacity as a system with an electromagnetic field [that is directly affected by our emotions].

Stress-reduction techniques at HeartMath have resulted in a dramatic reduction of cardiovascular-related problems. Simply by learning how to approach life's problems "creatively and proactively," that is, optimistically, participants have reported improved heart rhythm, decreased blood pressure, and reduction in medication. It seems that Pollyanna may have been on to something. The Glad Game could easily be regarded as a stress-reduction technique. In order to play it successfully, one has to replace negative emotions with positive ones and look at life "creatively and proactively" rather than as a helpless victim of the fates. When you are playing the Glad Game, you are forcing yourself not only to find the good in a potentially negative situation, but to expect that the good is always there. It's like playing hide and seek; good things may not always be immediately visible among the bad, but an adept Glad Game player will ferret them out and will come to trust implicitly in their existence. Therefore, it follows that worry and fear must eventually be replaced by hope and trust. Can you think of a better way to reduce stress and anxiety?

Some Glad Game Ideas

1. *Experience simultaneous realities.* What are you glad about at this very moment? If you are in pain, stop and think of anything in your life that is good, fun, or brings you joy. This practice alerts you to the fact that as an optimystic you are able, at any time, to experience seemingly contradictory emotions simultaneously. You can move in and out of feelings and moods; no one feeling is permanent, ever. You can be *glad* about that!

2. *Keep the humor coming.* In order to be successful at the glad game, a sense of humor is a must. This is a creative challenge, and creativity and humor always go together. Many people don't realize that *Pollyanna* is a humorous book, not a somber sermon. It is full of clever characterizations and funny situations, and one of its chief points is that when people stop seeing the fun in things, they stop living. When people's senses of humor and delight get rusty, Pollyanna is there to oil them.

3. *Get a glad game partner.* Playing with someone else can really get the glad game going. Find a willing partner, and devise a point system. The

worse the situation, the more points you get for finding something to be glad about. The goal is to basically try and out-glad your opponent— like the card game of War that we used to play as kids. You may find yourself in a hot debate over whose situation is the most dismal and why one or the other of you should win. Then, give extra points to whoever can be glad about having the argument. And remember, the one who loses also has to be glad she or he lost! You can play for anything— money, a dinner, a movie. Then you can be *really* glad you won!

4. *Keep a glad game observation journal.* Jot down things you're glad about when they occur to you. Then look over the journal when you're not feeling so glad.

5. *Keep on playing.* Remember, as with any game, the more you practice, the better you'll get at it. It's no coincidence that Pollyanna was the expert player in town. After all, she played the glad game all the time. You don't have to badger everybody with it, like she did. But if you simply want to adjust your gratitude attitude, to get into the optimystic spirit of gratefulness, it can be fun, challenging, and revealing. As Nancy, Miss Polly's overworked and underappreciated hired girl, reflects upon learning of Pollyanna's curious method of meeting and overcoming adversity, "If playin' a silly-fool game—about bein' glad you've got crutches when you want dolls—is got ter be—my way—o' bein' that rock o' refuge— why, I'm a-goin' ter play it—I am, I am!"

O 17

Go Out and Love Some More!

Optimysticism is not just a theory. Neither is it confined to the esoteric realms of spiritual or religious awakening. It is a practical way
of life that demands, by its very nature, to be shared with others, or
as the Zen masters would say, to be taken out into the marketplace.

While the mystic experience is always uniquely individual, the
optimystic experience is a communal exchange. As we get to know
our mystic selves, there is a certain amount of necessary going in-
ward, withdrawing from the world in order to be able to have an intimate, personal experience with the divine. But a relationship with
God is no different from a relationship with our fellow humans. In
fact, as we become optimystics, we discover that our relationship
with others becomes a direct extension of our relationship with
God. Therefore, our ultimate calling is to bring God, which translates to the spirit of love, hope, humor, and active compassion to
those with whom we come in contact. This does not mean preaching in the religious sense, but living in the spiritual sense, creating
a world of beauty and caring and respect that invites others to discover a comparable richness in themselves.

One of the ways to begin sharing the spirit of optimysticism is to
be willing to really experience life, and to communicate our experiences to others. This means being open to whatever we're handed,
and being wise enough not to run away from the experience but to

meet it head on, go where it takes us, discover its deeper meaning, and return from the journey to tell our tale, hopefully inspiring others to live as passionate, not passive, beings.

In the cult movie favorite *Harold and Maude,* twenty-year-old Harold admits to eighty-year-old Maude that he has spent most of his life dying. Maude, who has lived through many difficult experiences, including a sojourn in the concentration camps, responds as a cheerleader for life. She tells Harold to go out and live and play the game as well as he can, even to get hurt, because, after all, "If you don't play the game you'll have nothing to talk about in the locker room."

This is a good point, optimystically taken. We need to have something to talk about in the locker room. We need to have real experiences; we need to welcome the unknown, take risks, and continually test ourselves and our spirits so that when we return from our journeys we will have stories to tell that inspire others and attest to the fact that there is indeed life before death.

Stories are not difficult to find for those who make the decision to live in the spiritual moment. If we're optimystics, a trip to the grocery store can provide us with more stories, characters to talk about, and enthusiasm for life than our nonoptimystic neighbor's trip around the world. Life in any circumstance is a great adventure when we are awake.

Stories are very important to human life. When Nobel Prize–winning physicist Richard Feynman was in the final stages of dying from cancer, he was walking one day with one of his closest friends and students. The friend seemed sad; when Feynman asked him about it, he admitted that he was upset that Feynman was dying. Feynman agreed that it was sad, but then he said, "You know, I'll still be around, because I'm leaving lots of stories for people to tell. And so, every time there's a story, I'll be there!" And, it's true; there are great Feynman stories that will be told for a long, long time because he really played the game well. Through adversity, sickness, and heartbreaking loss, Feynman was an inspiration to everyone, a fun-filled, off-the-wall character who genuinely loved the game of life and radiated that zest to all who met him. Isn't this the way all of us would like to be remembered?

Although it might seem selfish or presumptuous to be happy in a world full of suffering, it's actually the opposite. It's not only okay to be hopeful and find happiness, it's our obligation. We are here not to suffer along with the suffering but to lift others up through compassion, to radiate hope by seeking out the meaning and beauty in life wherever we can. When, in *Harold and Maude,* Maude is dying and Harold cries out, "Maude, don't go—I love you!" Maude replies, "That's wonderful. Now, go out and love some more!"

All of us have a vital task on Earth: to keep beauty, peace, hope, love, laughter, caring, and happiness alive and well. Hope is as important as breathing; breathing with God brings us inspiration, and inspiration makes us one with both our joy and the whole of the human condition. The truly inspired person treats others with compassion, not judgment, and takes the time to really see things, not through the veil of preconception and opinion but through always open eyes. One optimystic practice that's guaranteed to keep you on your spiritual toes is to look at, look around, look through, look in, look sideways—in other words, to be on the lookout for another way of looking at things. The optimystic approach to life demands that we not limit our perception, that we become true visionaries, people who are able to see above, ahead, and beyond the limited dimension of everyday thinking. This is the imaginative way to live, the only way that has a chance of changing the planet for the better.

Optimysticism is a win/win proposition. The happier and more at peace we are, the happier and more at peace our environment becomes. It's global warming from another perspective. As optimystics, we cannot help but radiate joy and inspiration, because that's who we are: bearers of the light. The light of life, the lightness of being? This is the ray of hope with which optimystics can warm the world.

If ever there was a time for an optimystic revolution, it is now. As we approach the millennium, we may or may not be called upon to start this revolution. But it is certain that we will be called upon to create a new story, a mystic one, where the sacred is brought back to life and spiritual lessons are honored.

So we begin with ourselves. We tune in to our mystic self and grow more reflective, meditative, appreciative, and peaceful. We experience spiritual moments and lightness of spirit more and more frequently. We start to radiate joy and hope, regardless of our less-than-perfect circumstances. We begin to create an optimystic environment rich in color, beauty, laughter, courage, and compassion. We evolve to become more selfless and to practice true generosity. Others are drawn to our light. Joy begins to stir around us. When we die, we leave behind a glowing legacy of hope that continues to affect and inspire others. We are able to raise vibrations and transcend density. Now the world has become optimystic.

Is this fantasy—or possibility? Individual human beings are single sparks of divine fire that help to ignite and keep the flame of passion and compassion burning brightly in the heart of the universe. We know how our individual actions can become transformational power tools.

In closing, we thought it was appropriate, given the current fascination with styles of the 1960s and '70s, to resurrect what was probably the most popular manifesto of that period. It was found in Old St. Paul's Church in Baltimore, dated 1692. Somehow this simple document, a blessing to all those who seek to live fully, wisely, and with true spiritual intensity, hit a universal chord and spread through the public consciousness like a brushfire. If you're over thirty-five, you'll certainly remember the "Desiderata," which became so popular that there was hardly a wall, refrigerator, tourist trap, or coffee mug that didn't proclaim it. It became one of the biggest clichés of the counterculture years, yet it must have something to offer if it resonated so strongly with humanity nearly three hundred years after it was written. When we happened upon it recently, we realized that it is, in essence, the creed of the optimystic. And so we'd like to reprint it here and to encourage you to view it with your new pair of optimystic eyes.

Desiderata

Go placidly amid the noise and haste, and remember what peace there may be in silence. As far as possible without surrender be on good terms with all persons. Speak your truth quietly and clearly; and listen to others, even the dull and ignorant; they too have their story.

Avoid loud and aggressive persons; they are vexations to the spirit. If you compare yourself with others, you may become vain and bitter; for always there will be greater and lesser persons than yourself. Enjoy your achievements as well as your plans.

Keep interested in your own career, however humble; it is a real possession in the changing fortunes of time. Exercise caution in your business affairs; for the world is full of trickery. But let this not blind you to what virtue there is; many persons strive for high ideals; and everywhere life is full of heroism.

Be yourself. Especially, do not feign affection. Neither be cynical about love; for in the face of all aridity and disenchantment it is perennial as the grass.

Take kindly the counsel of the years, gracefully surrendering the things of youth. Nurture strength of spirit to shield you in sudden misfortune. But do not distress yourself with imaginings. Many fears are born of fatigue and loneliness. Beyond a wholesome discipline, be gentle with yourself.

You are a child of the universe, no less than the trees and the stars; you have a right to be here. And whether or not it is clear to you, no doubt the universe is unfolding as it should.

Therefore be at peace with God, whatever you conceive Him to be, and whatever your labors and aspirations, in the noisy confusion of life keep peace with your soul.

With all its sham, drudgery and broken dreams, it is still a beautiful world. Be careful. Strive to be happy.

And now, go out and love some more!

We would love to hear from you! Please write with any good news or optimystic experiences you would love to share for future books or newsletters. Feel free to share your impressions of the book, let us know what you like or don't like about *The Optimystic's Handbook*.

If you are interested in ordering audio tapes, and our other books, send a self-addressed stamped envelope.

Please let us know if you would be interested in a forthcoming *Optimystic's Newsletter*.

Please write; we love letters.

Thank you!

Direct all correspondence to:
Terry Lynn Taylor & Mary Beth Crain
Dancing Wheat Inc.
2275 Huntington Drive, #326
San Marino, CA 91108